SECOND
CHANCES

ALSO BY MAX LUCADO

SECOND
CHANCES

MORE
STORIES OF GRACE

MAX LUCADO

THOMAS NELSON
Since 1798

NASHVILLE   DALLAS   MEXICO CITY   RIO DE JANEIRO

Published in Nashville, Tennessee, by Thomas Nelson. Thomas Nelson is a registered trademark of Thomas Nelson, Inc.

Thomas Nelson, Inc., titles may be purchased in bulk for educational, business, fund-raising, or sales promotional use. For information, please e-mail SpecialMarkets@ThomasNelson.com.

ISBN 978-0-7852-3836-2 (IE)

Library of Congress Control Number: 2012955628

ISBN-13: 978-0-8499-4855-8

Printed in the United States of America

13 14 15 16 17 RRD 6 5 4 3 2 1

I DEDICATE THIS VOLUME TO
THE OAK HILLS CHURCH CAMPUS
MINISTERS AND THEIR LEADER, GREG
OEFINGER. MIGUEL FERIA, DAVIDA
LAMBERT, GREG LIGON, MICHAEL
MEEKS, AND RICH RONALD, THANK
YOU, MY FRIENDS. BECAUSE OF YOUR
HARD WORK, SECOND CHANCES ARE
HAPPENING EVERYWHERE!

CONTENTS

CONTENTS

INTRODUCTION

We humans are prone to failure, aren't we? We're experts at muddying, mixing, and messing up our lives. We've looked up from the bottom of a pit and realized we dug it ourselves; we've fallen so far we've wondered where to find hope.

Maybe you're like Moses, filled with regrets for a past you can't change. The shadow of sin shades the future, and you ask, "Could God do something with someone who's made such terrible mistakes?"

Or like Peter. You had it all together. You loved God and were ready to do battle for your Savior. But before the rooster crowed and the morning came, your faith faltered, and now you're knee-deep in a mire of your own making. Or perhaps you've been the one betrayed. Cheated on, stepped on, and overlooked, where do you go to escape the prison of bitterness? If you're drowning in regret, shamed by your mistakes, or unable to offer grace to the one who's wronged you, I hope you'll turn the page. And I pray you'll see your life experience in these stories. They remind us that there's forgiveness for past mistakes and hope for the future.

They are a witness to a God who specializes in second chances.

. . . FOR THE
REBELLIOUS

So this is what the LORD says:
"If you change your heart and return
to me, I will take you back.
Then you may serve me."

— JEREMIAH 15:19

· I ·

OPEN ARMS

Then Jesus said, "A man had two sons. The younger son said to his father, 'Give me my share of the property.' So the father divided the property between his two sons. Then the younger son gathered up all that was his and traveled far away to another country. There he wasted his money in foolish living. After he had spent everything, a time came when there was no food anywhere in the country, and the son was poor and hungry. So he got a job with one of the citizens there who sent the son into the fields to feed pigs. The son was so hungry that he wanted to eat the pods the pigs were eating, but no one gave him anything. When he realized what he was doing, he thought, 'All of my father's servants have plenty of food. But I am here, almost dying with hunger. I will leave and return to my father and say to him, "Father, I have sinned against God and against you. I am no longer worthy to be called your son, but let me be like one of your servants."' So the son left and went to his father.

"While the son was still a long way off, his father saw him and felt sorry for his son. So the father ran to him and

hugged and kissed him. The son said, 'Father, I have sinned against God and against you. I am no longer worthy to be called your son.' But the father said to his servants, 'Hurry! Bring the best clothes and put them on him. Also, put a ring on his finger and sandals on his feet. And get our fat calf and kill it so we can have a feast and celebrate. My son was dead, but now he is alive again! He was lost, but now he is found!' So they began to celebrate."

—LUKE 15:11-24

The boy stared at his reflection in the muddy puddle. He questioned whether the face was really his. It didn't look like him.

The flame in the eyes had been extinguished. The smirk had been humbled. The devil-may-care attitude had been replaced with soberness.

He tumbled headlong and landed face first.

It wasn't enough to be friendless. It wasn't enough to be broke. It wasn't enough to pawn his ring, his coat, even his shoes. The long hours walking the streets didn't break him. You would think that the nights with only a bunkhouse pillow or the days lugging a bucket of pig slop would force a change of heart.

But they didn't. Pride is made of stone. Hard knocks may chip it, but it takes reality's sledgehammer to break it.

His was beginning to crack.

His first few days of destitution were likely steamy with resentment. He was mad at everyone. Everyone was to blame. His friends shouldn't have bailed out on him. And his brother should come and bail him out. His boss should feed him better, and his dad never should have let him go in the first place.

He named a pig after each one of them. . . .

He could have done what millions do. He could have spent a lifetime in the pigpen pretending it was a palace. But he didn't.

Something told him that this was the moment of—and for—truth.

He looked into the water. The face he saw wasn't pretty—muddy and swollen. He looked away. "Don't think about it. You're no worse off than anybody else. Things will get better tomorrow."

The lies anticipated a receptive ear. They'd always found one before. "Not this time," he muttered. And he stared at his reflection.

"How far I have fallen." His first words of truth.

He looked into his own eyes. He thought of his father. "They always said I had your eyes." He could see the look of hurt on his father's face when he told him he was leaving.

"How I must have hurt you."

A crack zigzagged across the boy's heart.

A tear splashed into the pool. Another soon followed. Then another. Then the dam broke. He buried his face in his dirty hands as the tears did what tears do so well; they flushed out his soul.

His face was still wet as he sat near the pool. For the first time in a long time he thought of home. The memories warmed him. Memories of dinner-table laughter. Memories of a warm bed. Memories of evenings on the porch with his father as they listened to the hypnotic ring of the crickets.

"Father." He said the word aloud as he looked at himself. "They used to say I looked like you. Now you wouldn't even recognize me. Boy, I blew it, didn't I?"

He stood up and began to walk.

The road home was longer than he remembered. When he last traveled it, he turned heads because of his style. If he turned heads this time, it was because of his stink. His clothes were torn, his hair matted, and his feet black. But that didn't bother him, because for the first time in a calendar of heart-aches, he had a clean conscience.

He was going home. He was going home a changed man. Not demanding that he get what he deserved, but willing to take whatever he could get. "Give me" had been replaced with "help me," and his defiance had been replaced with repentance.

He came asking for everything with nothing to give in return. He had no money. He had no excuses.

And he had no idea how much his father had missed him.

He had no idea the number of times his father had paused between chores to look out the front gate for his son. The boy had no idea the number of times his father had awakened from restless sleep, gone into the son's room, and sat on the boy's bed. And the son would have never believed the hours the father had sat on the porch next to the empty rocking chair, looking, longing to see that familiar figure, that stride, that face.

As the boy came around the bend that led up to his house, he rehearsed his speech one more time.

"Father, I have sinned against heaven and against you."

He approached the gate and placed his hand on the latch. He began to lift it, then he paused. His plan to go home suddenly seemed silly. "What's the use?" he heard himself asking himself. "What chance do I have?" He ducked, turned around, and began to walk away.

Then he heard the footsteps. He heard the slap, slap, slap of sandals. Someone was running. He didn't turn to look. *It's probably a servant coming to chase me away or my big brother wanting to know what I'm doing back home.* He began to leave.

But the voice he heard was not the voice of a servant nor the voice of his brother; it was the voice of his father.

"Son!"

"Father?"

He turned to open the gate, but the father already had. The son looked at his father standing at the entrance. Tears glistened on his cheeks as arms stretched from east to west inviting the son to come home.

"Father, I have sinned." The words were muffled as the boy buried his face in his father's shoulder.

The two wept. For a forever they stood at the gate intertwined as one. Words were unnecessary. Repentance had been made; forgiveness had been given.

The boy was home.

If there is a scene in this story that deserves to be framed, it's the one of the father's outstretched hands. His tears are moving.

His smile is stirring. But his hands call us home. Imagine those hands. Strong fingers. Palms wrinkled with lifelines. Stretching open like a wide gate, leaving entrance as the only option.

When Jesus told this parable of the loving father, I wonder, did he use his hands? When he got to this point in the story, did he open his arms to illustrate the point?

Did he perceive the thoughts of those in the audience who were thinking, *I could never go home. Not after my life*? Did he see a housewife look at the ground and a businessman shake his head as if to say, "I can't start over. I've made too big a mess"? And did he open his arms even wider as if to say, "Yes. Yes, you can. You can come home"?

Whether he did that day or not, I don't know. But I know that he did later. He later stretched his hands as open as he could. He forced his arms so wide apart that it hurt. And to prove that those arms would never fold and those hands would never close, he had them nailed open.

They still are.

· 2 ·

COME HOME

Then Jesus told them this story: "Suppose one of you has a
hundred sheep but loses one of them. Then he will leave the
other ninety-nine sheep in the open field and go out and look
for the lost sheep until he finds it. And when he finds it, he
happily puts it on his shoulders and goes home. He calls to his
friends and neighbors and says, 'Be happy with me because I
found my lost sheep.' In the same way, I tell you there is more
joy in heaven over one sinner who changes his heart and life,
than over ninety-nine good people who don't need to change."

—LUKE 15:3-7

The practice of using earthly happenings to clarify heavenly truths is no easy task. Yet, occasionally, one comes across a story, legend, or fable that conveys a message as accurately as a hundred sermons and with ten times the creativity. Such is the case with the reading below. I heard it first told by a Brazilian preacher in São Paulo. And though I've shared it countless times, with each telling I am newly warmed and reassured by its message.

The small house was simple but adequate. It consisted of one large room on a dusty street. Its red-tiled roof was one of many in this poor neighborhood on the outskirts of the Brazilian village. It was a comfortable home. Maria and her daughter, Christina, had done what they could to add color to the gray walls and warmth to the hard dirt floor: an old calendar, a faded photograph of a relative, a wooden crucifix. The furnishings were modest: a pallet on either side of the room, a washbasin, and a wood-burning stove.

Maria's husband had died when Christina was an infant. The young mother, stubbornly refusing opportunities to remarry, got a job and set out to raise her young daughter. And now, fifteen years later, the worst years were over. Though Maria's salary as a maid afforded few luxuries, it was reliable and it did provide food and clothes. And now Christina was old enough to get a job to help out.

Some said Christina got her independence from her mother. She recoiled at the traditional idea of marrying young and raising a family. Not that she couldn't have had her pick of husbands. Her olive skin and brown eyes kept a steady stream of prospects at her door. She had an infectious way of throwing her head back and filling the room with laughter. She also had that rare magic some women have that makes every man feel like a king just by being near them. But it was her spirited curiosity that made her keep all the men at arm's length.

She spoke often of going to the city. She dreamed of trading her dusty neighborhood for exciting avenues and city life. Just the thought of this horrified her mother. Maria was always quick to remind Christina of the harshness of the streets. "People don't know you there. Jobs are scarce and the life is cruel. And besides, if you went there, what would you do for a living?"

Maria knew exactly what Christina would do, or would *have* to do for a living. That's why her heart broke when she awoke one morning to find her daughter's bed empty. Maria knew immediately where her daughter had gone. She also knew immediately what she must do to find her. She quickly threw some clothes in a bag, gathered up all her money, and ran out of the house.

On her way to the bus stop she entered a drugstore to get one last thing. Pictures. She sat in the photograph booth, closed the curtain, and spent all she could on pictures of herself. With her purse full of small black-and-white photos, she boarded the next bus to Rio de Janeiro.

Maria knew Christina had no way of earning money. She also knew that her daughter was too stubborn to give up. When pride meets hunger, a human will do things that were before unthinkable. Knowing this, Maria began her search. Bars, hotels, nightclubs, any place with the reputation for street walkers or prostitutes. She went to them all. And at each place she left her picture—taped on a bathroom mirror, tacked to a hotel bulletin board, fastened to a corner phone booth. And on the back of each photo she wrote a note.

It wasn't too long before both the money and the pictures

ran out, and Maria had to go home. The weary mother wept as the bus began its long journey back to her small village.

It was a few weeks later that Christina descended the hotel stairs. Her young face was tired. Her brown eyes no longer danced with youth but spoke of pain and fear. Her laughter was broken. Her dream had become a nightmare. A thousand times over she had longed to trade these countless beds for her secure pallet. Yet the little village was, in too many ways, too far away.

As she reached the bottom of the stairs, her eyes noticed a familiar face. She looked again, and there on the lobby mirror was a small picture of her mother. Christina's eyes burned and her throat tightened as she walked across the room and removed the small photo. Written on the back was this compelling invitation: "Whatever you have done, whatever you have become, it doesn't matter. Please come home."

She did.

· 3 ·

BRIGHT LIGHTS ON
DARK NIGHTS

The LORD caused a big fish to swallow Jonah, and Jonah was inside the fish three days and three nights.

   While Jonah was inside the fish, he prayed to the LORD his God and said,

   "When I was in danger,
      I called to the LORD,
      and he answered me.
   I was about to die,
      so I cried to you,
      and you heard my voice. . . .
   I will praise and thank you
      while I give sacrifices to you,
      and I will keep my promises to you.
   Salvation comes from the LORD!"

*Then the LORD spoke to the fish, and the fish threw up Jonah onto
the dry land.*

—JONAH 1:17–2:2, 2:9–10

G od has thrown life jackets to every generation.
Look at Jonah in the fish belly—surrounded by
gastric juices and sucked-in seaweed. For three days God has
left him there. For three days Jonah has pondered his choices.
And for three days he has come to the same conclusion: he ain't
got one. From where he sits (or floats) there are two exits—and
neither are very appealing. But then again, neither is Jonah. He
blew it as a preacher. He was a flop as a fugitive. At best he's a
coward, at worst a traitor. And what he's lacked all along he now
has in abundance—guts.

So Jonah does the only thing he can do: he prays. He says
nothing about how good he is—but a lot about how good God
is. He doesn't even ask for help, but help is what he gets. Before
he can say "amen," the belly convulses, the fish belches, and
Jonah lands face-first on the beach.

God's efforts are strongest when our efforts are useless.

I WILL NOT
ABANDON YOU

God has said,

> *"I will never leave you; I will never abandon you."*

—HEBREWS 13:5

F ive-year-old Madeline climbed into her father's lap.

"Did you have enough to eat?" he asked her.

She smiled and patted her tummy. "I can't eat any more."

"Did you have some of your grandma's pie?"

"A whole piece!"

Joe looked across the table at his mom. "Looks like you filled us up. Don't think we'll be able to do anything tonight but go to bed."

Madeline put her little hands on either side of his big face. "Oh, but, Poppa, this is Christmas Eve. You said we could dance."

Joe feigned a poor memory. "Did I now? Why, I don't remember saying anything about dancing."

Grandma smiled and shook her head as she began clearing the table.

"But, Poppa," Madeline pleaded, "we always dance on Christmas Eve. Just you and me, remember?"

A smile burst from beneath his thick mustache. "Of course I remember, darling. How could I forget?"

And with that he stood and took her hand in his, and for a moment, just a moment, his wife was alive again, and the two were walking into the den to spend another night before Christmas as they had spent so many, dancing away the evening.

They would have danced the rest of their lives, but then came the surprise pregnancy and the complications. Madeline survived. But her mother did not. And Joe, the thick-handed butcher from Minnesota, was left to raise his Madeline alone.

"Come on, Poppa." She tugged on his hand. "Let's dance before everyone arrives." She was right. Soon the doorbell would ring and the relatives would fill the floor and the night would be past.

But, for now, it was just Poppa and Madeline.

The love of a parent for a child is a mighty force. Consider the couple with their newborn child. The infant offers his parents absolutely nothing. No money. No skill. No words of wisdom. If he had pockets, they would be empty. To see an infant lying in a bassinet is to see utter helplessness. What is there to love?

Whatever it is, Mom and Dad find it. Just look at Mom's

face as she nurses her baby. Just watch Dad's eyes as he cradles the child. And just try to harm or speak evil of the infant. If you do, you'll encounter a mighty strength, for the love of a parent is a mighty force.

Jesus once asked, if we humans who are sinful have such a love, how much more does God, the sinless and selfless Father, love us?[1] But what happens when the love isn't returned? What happens to the heart of the father when his child turns away?

———◇◇———

Rebellion flew into Joe's world like a Minnesota blizzard. About the time she was old enough to drive, Madeline decided she was old enough to lead her life. And that life did not include her father.

"I should have seen it coming," Joe would later say, "but for the life of me I didn't." He didn't know what to do. He didn't know how to handle the pierced nose and the tight shirts. He didn't understand the late nights and the poor grades. And, most of all, he didn't know when to speak and when to be quiet.

She, on the other hand, had it all figured out. She knew when to speak to her father—never. She knew when to be quiet—always. The pattern was reversed, however, with the lanky, tattooed kid from down the street. He was no good, and Joe knew it.

And there was no way he was going to allow his daughter to spend Christmas Eve with that kid.

"You'll be with us tonight, young lady. You'll be at your grandma's house eating your grandma's pie. You'll be with us on Christmas Eve."

Though they were at the same table, they might as well have been on different sides of town. Madeline played with her food and said nothing. Grandma tried to talk to Joe, but he was in no mood to chat. Part of him was angry; part of him was heartbroken. And the rest of him would have given anything to know how to talk to this girl who once sat on his lap.

Soon the relatives arrived, bringing with them a welcome end to the awkward silence. As the room filled with noise and people, Joe stayed on one side, Madeline sat sullenly on the other.

"Put on the music, Joe," reminded one of his brothers. And so he did. Thinking she would be honored, he turned and walked toward his daughter. "Will you dance with your poppa tonight?"

The way she huffed and turned, you'd have thought he'd insulted her. In full view of the family, she walked out the front door and marched down the sidewalk. Leaving her father alone.

Very much alone.

⬥

According to the Bible we have done the same. We have spurned the love of our Father. "Each of us has gone his own way" (Isa. 53:6).

Paul takes our rebellion a step further. We have done more than turn away, he says; we have turned *against*. "We were living against God" (Rom. 5:6).

He speaks even more bluntly in verse 10: "We were God's enemies." Harsh words, don't you think? An enemy is an adversary. One who offends, not out of ignorance, but by intent. Does this describe us? Have we ever been enemies of God? Have we ever turned against our Father?

Have you . . .

> ever done something, knowing God wouldn't want you
> to do it?
>
> ever hurt one of his children or part of creation?
>
> ever supported or applauded the work of his adversary,
> the devil?
>
> ever turned against your heavenly Father in public?

If so, have you not taken the role of an enemy?

So how does God react when we become his enemies?

———◇◇◇———

Madeline came back that night but not for long. Joe never faulted her for leaving. After all, what's it like being the daughter of a butcher? In their last days together he tried so hard. He made her favorite dinner—she didn't want to eat. He invited her to a movie—she stayed in her room. He bought her a new dress—she didn't even say thank you. And then there was that spring day he left work early to be at the house when she arrived home from school.

Wouldn't you know that was the day she never came home.

A friend saw her and her boyfriend in the vicinity of the bus station. The authorities confirmed the purchase of a ticket to Chicago; where she went from there was anybody's guess.

———◇◇◇———

The most notorious road in the world is the Via Dolorosa, the "Way of Sorrows." According to tradition, it is the route Jesus took from Pilate's hall to Calvary. The path is marked by stations frequently used by Christians for their devotions. One station marks the passing of Pilate's verdict. Another, the appearance of Simon to carry the cross. Two stations commemorate the stumble of Christ, another the words of Christ. There are fourteen stations in all, each one a reminder of the events of Christ's final journey.

Is the route accurate? Probably not. When Jerusalem was destroyed in A.D. 70 and again in A.D. 135, the streets of the city were destroyed. As a result, no one knows the exact route Christ followed that Friday.

But we do know where the path actually began.

The path began, not in the court of Pilate, but in the halls of heaven. The Father began his journey when he left his home in search of us. Armed with nothing more than a passion to win your heart, he came looking. His desire was singular—to bring his children home. The Bible has a word for this quest: *reconciliation*.

"God was in Christ reconciling the world to Himself" (2 Cor. 5:19 NKJV). The Greek word for *reconcile* means "to render something otherwise."[2] Reconciliation restiches the unraveled, reverses the rebellion, rekindles the cold passion.

Reconciliation touches the shoulder of the wayward and woos him homeward.

The path to the cross tells us exactly how far God will go to call us back.

The scrawny boy with the tattoos had a cousin. The cousin worked the night shift at a convenience store south of Houston. For a few bucks a month, he would let the runaways stay in his apartment at night, but they had to be out during the day.

Which was fine with them. They had big plans. He was going to be a mechanic, and Madeline just knew she could get a job at a department store. Of course he knew nothing about cars, and she knew even less about getting a job—but you don't think of things like that when you're intoxicated on freedom.

After a couple of weeks, the cousin changed his mind. And the day he announced his decision, the boyfriend announced his. Madeline found herself facing the night with no place to sleep or hand to hold.

It was the first of many such nights.

A woman in the park told her about the homeless shelter near the bridge. For a couple of bucks she could get a bowl of soup and a cot. A couple of bucks was about all she had. She used her backpack as a pillow and jacket as a blanket. The room was so rowdy it was hard to sleep. Madeline turned her face to the wall and, for the first time in several days, thought of the whiskered face of her father as he would kiss her good night. But as her eyes began to water, she refused to cry. She pushed the memory deep inside and determined not to think about home.

She'd gone too far to go back.

The next morning the girl in the cot beside her showed her a fistful of tips she'd made from dancing on tables. "This is the last night I'll have to stay here," she said. "Now I can pay for my own place. They told me they are looking for another girl. You should come by." She reached into her pocket and pulled out a matchbook. "Here's the address."

Madeline's stomach turned at the thought. All she could do was mumble, "I'll think about it."

She spent the rest of the week on the streets looking for work. At the end of the week when it was time to pay her bill at the shelter, she reached into her pocket and pulled out the matchbook. It was all she had left.

"I won't be staying tonight," she said and walked out the door.

Hunger has a way of softening convictions.

———◇◇◇———

Pride and shame. You'd never know they are sisters. They appear so different. Pride puffs out her chest. Shame hangs her head. Pride boasts. Shame hides. Pride seeks to be seen. Shame seeks to be avoided.

But don't be fooled, the emotions have the same parentage. And the emotions have the same impact. They keep you from your Father.

Pride says, "You're too good for him."

Shame says, "You're too bad for him."

Pride drives you away.

Shame keeps you away.

If pride is what goes before a fall, then shame is what keeps you from getting up after one.

———◇◇◇———

If Madeline knew anything, she knew how to dance. Her father had taught her. Now men the age of her father watched her. She didn't rationalize it—she just didn't think about it. Madeline simply did her work and took their dollars.

She might have never thought about it, except for the letters. The cousin brought them. Not one, or two, but a box full. All addressed to her. All from her father.

"Your old boyfriend must have squealed on you. These come two or three a week," complained the cousin. "Give him your address." Oh, but she couldn't do that. He might find her.

Nor could she bear to open the envelopes. She knew what they said; he wanted her home. But if he knew what she was doing, he would not be writing.

It seemed less painful not to read them. So she didn't. Not that week, nor the next when the cousin brought more, nor the next when he came again. She kept them in the dressing room at the club, organized according to postmark. She ran her finger over the top of each but couldn't bring herself to open one.

Most days Madeline was able to numb the emotions. Thoughts of home and thoughts of shame were shoved into the same part of her heart. But there were occasions when the thoughts were too strong to resist.

Like the time she saw a dress in the clothing store window. A dress the same color as one her father had purchased for her. A dress that had been far too plain for her. With much reluctance she had put it on and stood with him before the mirror. "My, you are as tall as I am," he had told her. She had stiffened at his touch.

Seeing her weary face reflected in the store window, Madeline realized she'd give a thousand dresses to feel his arm again. She left the store and resolved not to pass by it again.

In time the leaves fell and the air chilled. The mail came and the cousin complained and the stack of letters grew. Still she refused to send him an address. And she refused to read a letter.

Then a few days before Christmas Eve another letter arrived. Same shape. Same color. But this one had no postmark. And it was not delivered by the cousin. It was sitting on her dressing room table.

"A couple of days ago a big man stopped by and asked me to give this to you," explained one of the other dancers. "Said you'd understand the message."

"He was here?" she asked anxiously.

The woman shrugged, "Suppose he had to be."

Madeline swallowed hard and looked at the envelope. She opened it and removed the card. "I know where you are," it read. "I know what you do. This doesn't change the way I feel. What I've said in each letter is still true."

"But I don't know what you've said," Madeline declared. She pulled a letter from the top of the stack and read it. Then a second and a third. Each letter had the same sentence. Each sentence asked the same question.

In a matter of moments the floor was littered with paper and her face was streaked with tears.

Within an hour she was on a bus. "I just might make it in time." She barely did.

The relatives were starting to leave. Joe was helping Grandma in the kitchen when his brother called from the suddenly quiet den. "Joe, someone is here to see you."

Joe stepped out of the kitchen and stopped. In one hand the girl held a backpack. In the other she held a card. Joe saw the question in her eyes.

"The answer is yes," she said to her father. "If the invitation is still good, the answer is yes."

Joe swallowed hard. "Oh my. The invitation is good."

And so the two danced again on Christmas Eve.

On the floor, near the door, rested a letter with Madeline's name and her father's request.

"Will you come home and dance with your poppa again?"

THE GOLDEN GOBLET

Now the snake was the most clever of all the wild animals the LORD God had made. One day the snake said to the woman, "Did God really say that you must not eat fruit from any tree in the garden?"

The woman answered the snake, "We may eat fruit from the trees in the garden. But God told us, 'You must not eat fruit from the tree that is in the middle of the garden. You must not even touch it, or you will die.'"

But the snake said to the woman, "You will not die. God knows that if you eat the fruit from that tree, you will learn about good and evil and you will be like God!"

The woman saw that the tree was beautiful, that its fruit was good to eat, and that it would make her wise. So she took some of its fruit and ate it. She also gave some of the fruit to her husband who was with her, and he ate it.

— GENESIS 3:1–6

Flames leap from the hill. Pillows of smoke float upward. Orange tongues crack and pop.

From the midst of the blaze comes a yell—the protest of a prisoner as the dungeon door is locked; the roar of a lion as he feels the heat of the burning jungle.

The cry of a lost son as he looks for his father.

"My God, my God, why have you forsaken me?"

The words ricochet from star to star, crashing into the chamber of the King. Couriers from a bloody battlefield, they stumble into the King's presence. Bruised and broken, they plea for help, for relief.

The soldiers of the King prepare to attack. They mount their steeds and position their shields. They draw their swords.

But the King is silent. It is the hour for which he has planned. He knows his course of action. He has awaited those words since the beginning—since the first poison was smuggled into the kingdom.

It came camouflaged. It came in a golden cup with a long stem. It was in the flavor of fruit. It came not in the hands of a king, but the hands of a prince—the prince of the shadows.

Until this moment there had been no reason to hide in the Garden. The King walked with his children, and the children knew their King. There were no secrets. There were no shadows.

Then the prince of shadows entered the Garden. He had to hide himself. He was too ugly, too repulsive. Craters marred his face. So he came in darkness. He came encircled in ebony. He was completely hidden; only his voice could be heard.

"Taste it," he whispered, holding the goblet before her. "It's sweet with wisdom."

The daughter heard the voice and turned. She was intrigued. Her eyes had never seen a shadow. There was something tantalizing about his hiddenness.

The King watched. His army knew the prince of shadows would be no contest for their mighty legion. Eagerly they awaited the command to attack.

But no command was given.

"The choice is hers," the King instructed. "If she turns to us for help, that is your command to deliver her. If she doesn't turn, if she doesn't look to me—don't. The choice is hers."

The daughter stared at the goblet. Rubies embedded in gold filigree invited her touch. Wine wooed her to taste. She reached out and took the cup and drank the poison. Her eyes never looked up.

The venom rushed through her, distorting her vision, scarring her skin, and twisting her heart. She ducked into the shadow of the prince.

Suddenly she was lonely. She missed the intimacy she was made to know. Yet rather than return to the King, she chose to lure another away from him. She replenished the goblet and offered it to the son.

Once again the army snapped into position. Once again they listened for the command of the King. His words were the same. "If he looks to me, then rush to him. If he doesn't, then don't go. The choice is his."

The daughter placed the goblet into the hands of the son.

"It's all right," she assured. "It's sweet." The son looked at the delight that danced in her eyes. Behind her stood a silhouetted figure.

"Who is he?" the son asked.

"Drink it," she insisted. Her voice was husky with desire.

The goblet was cold against Adam's lips. The liquid burned his innocence. "More?" he requested as he ran his finger through the dregs on the bottom and put it to his mouth.

The soldiers looked to their King for instructions. His eyes were moist.

"Bring me your sword!" The general dismounted and stepped quickly toward the throne. He extended the unsheathed blade before the King.

The King didn't take it; he merely touched it. As the tip of his finger encountered the top of the sword, the iron grew orange with heat. It grew brighter and brighter until it blazed.

The general held the fiery sword and awaited the King's command. It came in the form of an edict.

"Their choice will be honored. Where there is poison, there will be death. Where there are goblets, there will be fire. Let it be done."

The general galloped to the Garden and took his post at the gate. The flaming sword proclaimed that the kingdom of light would never again be darkened by the passing of shadows. The King hated the shadows. He hated them because in the shadows the children could not see their King. The King hated the goblets. He hated them because they made the children forget the Father.

But outside the Garden the circle of the shadow grew larger and more empty goblets littered the ground. More faces were disfigured. More eyes saw distortedly. More souls were twisted. Purity was forgotten, and all sight of the King was lost. No one remembered that once there was a kingdom without shadows.

In their hands were the goblets of selfishness.

On their lips was the litany of the liar. "Taste it; it's sweet."

And, true to the words of the King, where there was poison, there was death. Where there were goblets, there was fire. Until the day the King sent his Prince.

The same fire that ignited the sword now lit a candle and placed it amidst the shadows.

His arrival, like that of the goblet bearer, did not go unnoticed.

"A star!" was how his coming was announced. "A bright light in a dark sky." A diamond glittering in the dirt.

"Burn brightly, my Son," whispered the King.

Many times the Prince of Light was offered the goblet. Many times it came in the hands of those who'd abandoned the King. "Just a taste, my friend?" With anguish Jesus would look into the eyes of those who tried to tempt him. What is this poison that would make a prisoner try to kill the one who came to release him?

The goblet still bore the seductive flavor of promised power and pleasure. But to the Son of Light its odor was vile. The very sight of the goblet so angered the Prince that he knocked it out of the hand of the tempter, leaving the two alone, locked in an intense glare.

"I will taste the poison," swore the King's Son. "For this I have come. But the hour will be mine to choose."

Finally that hour came. The Son went for one last visit with his Father. He met him in another garden. A garden of gnarled trees and stony soil.

"Does it have to be this way?"

"It does."

"Is there no one else who can do it?"

The King swallowed. "None but you."

"Do I have to drink from the cup?"

"Yes, my Child. The same cup."

He looked at the Prince of Light. "The darkness will be great." He passed his hand over the spotless face of his Son. "The pain will be awful." Then he paused and looked at his darkened dominion. When he looked up, his eyes were moist. "But there is no other way."

The Son looked into the stars as he heard the answer. "Then, let it be done."

Slowly the words that would kill the Son began to come from the lips of the Father.

"Hour of death, moment of sacrifice, it is your moment. Rehearsed a million times on false altars with false lambs, the moment of truth has come.

"Soldiers, you think you lead him? Ropes, you think you bind him? Men, you think you sentence him? He heeds not your commands. He winces not at your lashes. It is my voice he obeys. It is my condemnation he dreads. And it is your souls he saves.

"Oh, my Son, my Child. Look up into the heavens and see my face before I turn it. Hear my voice before I silence it. Would that I could save you and them. But they don't see and they don't hear.

"The living must die so that the dying can live. The time has come to kill the Lamb.

"Here is the cup, my Son. The cup of sorrows. The cup of sin.

"Slam, mallet! Be true to your task. Let your ring be heard throughout the heavens.

"Lift him, soldiers. Lift him high to his throne of mercy. Lift him up to his perch of death. Lift him above the people that curse his name.

"Now plunge the tree into the earth. Plunge it deep into the heart of humanity. Deep into the strata of time past. Deep into the seeds of time future.

"Is there no angel to save my Isaac? Is there no hand to redeem the Redeemer?

"Here is the cup, my Son. Drink it alone."

God must have wept as he performed his task. Every lie, every lure, every act done in shadows was in that cup. Slowly, hideously they were absorbed into the body of the Son. The final act of incarnation.

The Spotless Lamb was blemished. Flames began to lick his feet.

The King obeys his own edict. "Where there is poison, there will be death. Where there are goblets, there will be fire."

The King turns away from his Prince. The undiluted wrath of a sin-hating Father falls upon his sin-filled Son. The fire envelops him. The shadow hides him. The Son looks for his Father, but his Father cannot be seen.

"My God, my God . . . why?"

The throne room is dark and cavernous. The eyes of the King are closed. He is resting.

In his dream he is again in the Garden. The cool of the evening floats across the river as the three walk. They speak of the Garden—of how it is, of how it will be.

"Father . . ." the Son begins. The King replays the word again. Father. Father. The word was a flower, petal-delicate, yet so easily crushed. Oh, how he longed for his children to call him Father again.

A noise snaps him from his dream. He opens his eyes and sees a transcendent figure gleaming in the doorway. "It is finished, Father. I have come home."

· 6 ·

NEARER THAN
YOU'VE DREAMED

Come near to God, and God will come near to you.

—JAMES 4:8

B entley Bishop stepped out of the elevator into a buzz of activity, all directed at him. The first voice was the urgent one of Eric, his producer.

"Mr. Bishop, I've been trying to reach you for the last two hours." Eric simmered with nervous energy. He stood a couple of inches over five feet in a wrinkled suit, loose tie, and the same scuffed loafers he'd worn for the last year. Though he was barely thirty, his hairline had retreated halfway and appeared on pace to soon evacuate the dome. His fashion turned no heads. But his media savvy did.

Eric read society like a radar screen. Departing fads, incoming trends, who teens followed, what executives ate—Eric knew the culture. As a result, he knew talk shows. He knew the hot topics, the best guests, and Bentley Bishop knew his show was in good hands with Eric. Even if he was prone to panic.

"I never carry a phone on the golf course, Eric. You know that."

"Didn't the pro shop tell you I'd called?"

"They did." By now the makeup artist was tying a bib around Bishop's neck. "Did I get some sun today, honey?" he asked, sizing her up with a head-to-toe look. She was young enough to be his daughter, but his glance wasn't paternal. "Then again, the red face may be your fault, Meagan. Seeing you always makes me blush."

Bishop's flirting repulsed everyone but Bishop. The production crew had seen him do the same with a dozen other girls. The two receptionists cut their eyes at each other. He used to sweet-talk them. Now he toyed with the "sweet thing in the tight jeans," or so they had heard him describe her.

Eric would fire Meagan in a heartbeat, but he didn't have the authority. Meagan would leave in half a heartbeat, but she needed the money.

"Mr. Bishop." Eric scowled, looking at his watch. "We've got a problem."

From down the hall came the announcement. "Fifteen minutes to air."

"Oops." Bishop winked, untying the makeup bib. "Looks like we'll have to finish this later, babe."

Meagan powdered his cheek one final time and forced a smile.

"Dr. Allsup canceled," Eric inserted as the two headed for the studio.

"What?"

"Weather. He called from O'Hare."

"The Midwest is having weather problems?"

"Apparently Chicago is."

The two stopped in the middle of the hallway, and for the first time, Bishop gave Eric his full attention. He loomed over his producer by a full foot, his mane of thick white hair making him look even taller. Everyone in America, it seemed, recognized that square jaw and those caterpillar eyebrows. Twenty years of nightly interviews had elevated him to billboard status.

"What's our topic?" he asked.

"Surviving stress."

"Appropriate. Did you phone some fill-ins?"

"I did."

"Dr. Varner?"

"Sick."

"Dr. Chambers?"

"Out of town."

"What about those two guys we had last month who wrote that breathing book?"

"*Breathe Right, Live Right.* One has a cold. The other didn't call back."

"Then we're stuck with the rabbi."

"He's out too."

"Rabbi Cohen? He's never out. He's been subbing for ten years."

"Fifteen. His sister died and he's in Topeka."

"So where does that leave us? Doing a remote? I don't like remotes." By now Bishop's voice was beginning to boom and Eric's face to redden. The ninth-floor hallway of the Burbank Plaza Building was silent—busy, but silent. No one envied Eric.

"No remote, Mr. Bishop. The system is down."

"What?"

"Lightning from last night's storm."

"Did we have a storm last night?" Bishop asked everyone in hearing distance.

Eric shrugged. "I had us hooked up with the president's physician, then discovered the technical problems. No outside feeds."

The smile had long since vanished from Bishop's face. "No guests. No feeds. Why didn't you call me?"

Eric knew better than to answer honestly.

"Studio audience?"

"Packed. They came to see Dr. Allsup."

"So what do we do?" Bishop demanded.

"Ten minutes!" came a voice.

"We have a guest," Eric explained, slowly turning toward the studio door. "He's already in makeup."

"Where did you find him?"

"I think he found us." By now they were walking fast. "He sent me an e-mail an hour ago."

"How did he get your e-mail address?"

"I don't know. Nor do I know how he found out about our situation, but he did." Eric pulled a piece of paper from his jacket side pocket. "He told me he's sorry about Varner, Chambers, the

38

Chicago weather, and last night's lightning. But he didn't like the breathing book anyway. And, knowing our plight, he volunteered to do the show."

"That's crazy." Eric opened the door. Bishop entered, never losing eye contact with Eric. "You let him in?"

"Actually, he sort of let himself in. But I called around. He's causing quite a stir, mainly in smaller markets. Teaches ethics at a junior college near Birmingham. Some religious leaders are concerned, but the rank and file like him. He lectures at colleges, popular on the banquet circuit. Talks a lot about finding peace in your soul."

By now Bishop was stepping toward the set. "I could use some peace. Hope this guy's good. What's his name?"

"Jesse. Jesse Carpenter."

"Never heard of him. Let's give him fifteen minutes. For the last half of the program, rerun the highlight show."

"But we did that last week."

"People forget. Go to makeup and check on this Carpenter fellow."

<hr />

Meagan could see both her face and Jesse's in the mirror. She would later describe him as nice looking but not heart stopping. He wore a brown, elbow-patched corduroy coat, khaki slacks, and an acceptable but forgettable tie. A straight part separated his hair on the side, giving it a just-cut look. Meagan tied the apron around his neck and began with polite chitchat. His smile required no coaxing.

"First time on the show?"

"Yes."

"First time to the West Coast?"

"You might say that."

Meagan dabbed base powder on his cheeks, then stopped. He was staring at her. "Is this required?" he asked. He wasn't enjoying the drill.

"Keeps the glare down," she explained.

As she powdered, Jesse closed his eyes, then opened them and looked at her, saying nothing.

Meagan wondered about him. When men stared at her, she knew what they wanted. He's probably the same. She stepped behind the chair and sprayed his hair. He closed his eyes again. She looked at herself, curious what he might think of her—tattooed rose on her neck, jet-black hair and fingernails. T-shirt tied tight in the back, leaving her stomach exposed. A far cry from her role as a majorette in the high-school band. Her older brother, who managed the family pharmacy in Missouri, was always calling and asking, "You're not getting a tattoo, are you? And keep those rings out of your nose." She didn't listen.

She really didn't care what he thought. After all, she was twenty-one. Can't a girl have a life?

"Architecture?"

The one-word question caught Meagan off guard. "What?"

Jesse had opened his eyes, and with them he gestured to her open backpack that sat on the counter. A copy of *Architectural Digest* leaned out.

"Call it a secret interest," she explained. "Who knows, someday . . ."

"Have any other secrets?"

Meagan sighed. Of all the come-ons. "None that you need to hear about." She shrugged.

Men never ceased to amaze her. Her mother's warning was right: no matter how nice they look, first the line, then the hook. For a couple of minutes neither spoke. Meagan liked it that way. She found safety in silence. Jesse, however, wasn't finished.

"Bishop asks a lot of you."

Meagan cocked her head. "Is that a question?"

"No, just the truth."

"He's all right." Meagan sidestepped the topic, intentionally avoiding Jesse's eyes as she dusted his forehead one last time.

Jesse's tone was solemn. "Meagan, don't let your heart get hard. You were not made to be this edgy, this crusty."

She dropped her hands to her side and looked at Jesse, at first offended, then curious.

"What do you know about me?"

"I know you are a better person than this. I also know it's not too late to make a change. This street you're traveling? The houses look nice, but the road goes nowhere."

She started to object, but his eyes caught hers. "I can help, Meagan. I really can."

"I don't need your help" were the words she started to say, but didn't. He smiled softly, reassuringly. More silence followed. Not awkward. Just silence. Meagan felt a smile forming in reply, but then . . .

"Five minutes!" shouted a studio voice. Meagan looked up to see Eric's face.

Meagan never watched the *Bentley Bishop Show*. The first couple of days she had tried but quickly grew weary of his piano-key smile and disc-jockey voice. So she lost interest. She tried chatting with other staff members, but they knew how she got and kept her job. Show veterans formed a tight club, and girls like Meagan needn't apply for membership. "You'd think I was a leper," she'd mumbled after her final attempt at conversation.

Meagan followed her daily ritual of cleaning her counter, pulling out her magazine, and sitting in the makeup chair. But on this day, as she lifted the remote to turn off the makeup-room monitor, she saw Jesse walk out on stage.

People offered polite applause. She watched Jesse greet the host, take his seat, and nod at the crowd. Bishop turned his attention to the index cards resting on the table, each bearing an Eric-prepared question. He gave them a shuffle and set things in motion.

"Tell us about yourself, Mr. Carpenter. I understand you teach at a community college."

"Night courses mainly."

"In Alabama?"

"Yessir. Sawgrass, Alabama."

"Do people in Sawgrass know the meaning of stress?"

Jesse nodded.

Bishop continued: "This is a tough, tough world, Jesse.

Brutally competitive, highly demanding. Tell us, how do we handle the stress?"

The teacher sat up a bit straighter, made a tent with his hands, and began to speak. "Stress signals a deeper need, a longing. We long to fit in, to make a difference. Acceptance, significance—these matter to us. So we do what it takes; we go into debt to buy the house, we stretch the credit card to buy the clothes . . . and life on the treadmill begins."

"Treadmill?"

"Right, we spend a lot of energy going nowhere. At the end of the day, or the end of a life, we haven't moved one step. We're stuck."

"What do we do about it?"

"What we *typically* do doesn't work. We take vacations. We take pills. We take our chances in Vegas. We take advantage of younger women . . ." Jesse looked straight at Bishop as he spoke. But if Bishop connected the dots, he didn't show it.

Meagan did, and for the first time in a long time, she smiled.

"Doesn't work, Mr. Bishop. Back home we call it 'sipping out of the swamp.' There's stuff in that water we were never made to drink." This time Jesse turned toward the camera.

For a moment Meagan felt as if he were speaking to her, just to her. In self-defense, she muted the sound and watched him speak.

His minutes on the show totaled no more than seven. She later heard that Bishop and Eric were pleased, even interested in asking him to return.

She hoped they would.

———◇◇◇———

Jesse spotted Meagan through the window of a café, squeezing lemon into her glass of water. For a couple of minutes he watched. The restaurant had a retro look, a throwback to diner days with soda counters and silver-rimmed tables. Two men in an adjacent booth said something to her; she ignored them. A server offered her a menu; she declined it. A car screeched to a stop and honked at a jaywalking pedestrian; she looked up. That's when Meagan saw him.

Jesse smiled. She didn't. But neither did she turn away. She watched him cross the narrow street, enter the café, and walk toward her booth. He asked if he could join her, and she nodded. As he signaled the server, Meagan noticed Jesse looked tired.

He said little as he waited on his coffee. She spoke even less, at first. But once she began, her whole story tumbled out. Dropped by a boyfriend in Missouri. Fed up with her family. Someone told her she could make fast money in commercials. Escaped to the West Coast. Audition after audition. Rejection after rejection. Finally cosmetics school. "I never even finished," she confessed. "I heard about the opening at Bentley Bishop's. Went for an interview and . . ."—she looked away—"after doing what he wanted, he hired me. And now"—a tear bubbled—"I'm here. I pay the rent and don't go hungry. Twenty-one years old and surviving L.A. Sounds like the chorus of a country-western song. But I'm okay. At least that's what I tell myself."

Jesse's sandwich arrived. He offered her half, but she declined. After a couple of bites, he wiped his mouth with a napkin.

"Meagan, I know you. I've watched you stain pillows with tears and walk streets because you couldn't sleep. I know you. And I know you hate who you are becoming."

"So"—Meagan touched the corner of her eye with the back of a knuckle—"if you're such a psychic, tell me: where's God in all this? I've been looking for him a long, long time." With a sudden increase in volume, she began listing misdeeds on her fingers. "I ran out on my folks. I sleep with my boss. I've spent more time on a barstool than a church pew. I'm tired, tired of it all." She bit her lip and looked away.

Jesse inclined the same direction and caught her attention. She looked up to see him beaming, energetic, as though he were an algebra professor and she were struggling with two plus two.

"Where is God in all this?" He repeated her question. "Nearer than you've ever dreamed." He took her glass and held it. "Meagan, everyone who drinks this water will get thirsty again. But I offer a different drink. Anyone who drinks the water I give will never thirst. Not ever."

Again, silence.

With a finger Meagan bounced the ice cubes in the glass. Finally she asked, "Never?"

"Not ever."

She looked away, then looked back, and, with every ounce of honesty she owned, asked, "Tell me, Jesse. Who in the world are you?"

Her new friend leaned forward in response and replied, "I thought you'd never ask."

. . . FOR THE
REGRET-RIDDLED

The Son of Man came to find lost
people and save them.

—LUKE 19:10

· 7 ·

TWO TOMBSTONES

When a Samaritan woman came to the well to get some water, Jesus said to her, "Please give me a drink." (This happened while Jesus' followers were in town buying some food.)

The woman said, "I am surprised that you ask me for a drink, since you are a Jewish man and I am a Samaritan woman." (Jewish people are not friends with Samaritans.)

Jesus said, ". . . Everyone who drinks this water will be thirsty again, but whoever drinks the water I give will never be thirsty. The water I give will become a spring of water gushing up inside that person, giving eternal life."

The woman said to him, "Sir, give me this water so I will never be thirsty again and will not have to come back here to get more water."

Jesus told her, "Go get your husband and come back here."

The woman answered, "I have no husband."

Jesus said to her, "You are right to say you have no

husband. Really you have had five husbands, and the man
you live with now is not your husband. You told the truth."

The woman said, "Sir, I can see that you are a prophet.
Our ancestors worshiped on this mountain, but you say that
Jerusalem is the place where people must worship."

Jesus said, ". . . God is spirit, and those who worship
him must worship in spirit and truth."

The woman said, "I know that the Messiah is coming."
(Messiah is the One called Christ.) "When the Messiah
comes, he will explain everything to us."

Then Jesus said, "I am he—I, the one talking to
you.". . .

Then the woman left her water jar and went back to
town. She said to the people, "Come and see a man who
told me everything I ever did. Do you think he might be the
Christ?"

—JOHN 4:7-10, 13-21, 24-26, 28-29

I had driven by the place countless times. Daily I passed the
small plot of land on the way to my office. Daily I told
myself, *Someday I need to stop there.*

Today, that "someday" came. I convinced a tight-fisted sched-
ule to give me thirty minutes, and I drove in.

The intersection appears no different from any other in San

Antonio: a Burger King, a Rodeway Inn, a restaurant. But turn northwest, go under the cast-iron sign, and you will find yourself on an island of history that is holding its own against the river of progress.

The name on the sign? Locke Hill Cemetery.

As I parked, a darkened sky threatened rain. A lonely path invited me to walk through the two-hundred-plus tombstones. The fatherly oak trees arched above me, providing a ceiling for the solemn chambers. Tall grass, still wet from the morning dew, brushed my ankles.

The tombstones, though weathered and chipped, were alive with yesterday.

Ruhet in herrn accents the markers that bear names like Schmidt, Faustman, Grundmeyer, and Eckert.

Ruth Lacey is buried there. Born in the days of Napoleon—1807. Died over a century ago—1877.

I stood on the same spot where a mother wept on a cold day some eight decades past. The tombstone read simply, "Baby Boldt—Born and died December 10, 1910."

Eighteen-year-old Harry Ferguson was laid to rest in 1883 under these words: "Sleep sweetly tired young pilgrim." I wondered what wearied him so.

Then I saw it. It was chiseled into a tombstone on the northern end of the cemetery. The stone marks the destination of the body of Grace Llewellen Smith. No date of birth is listed, no date of death. Just the names of her two husbands, and this epitaph:

Sleeps, but rests not.
Loved, but was loved not.
Tried to please, but pleased not.
Died as she lived—alone.

Words of futility.

I stared at the marker and wondered about Grace Llewellen Smith. I wondered about her life. I wondered if she'd written the words . . . or just lived them. I wondered if she deserved the pain. I wondered if she was bitter or beaten. I wondered if she was plain. I wondered if she was beautiful. I wondered why some lives are so fruitful while others are so futile.

I caught myself wondering aloud, "Mrs. Smith, what broke your heart?"

Raindrops smudged my ink as I copied the words.

Loved, but was loved not . . .

Long nights. Empty beds. Silence. No response to messages left. No return to letters written. No love exchanged for love given.

Tried to please, but pleased not . . .

I could hear the hatchet of disappointment.

"How many times do I have to tell you?" Chop.

"You'll never amount to anything." Chop. Chop.

"Why can't you do anything right?" Chop, chop, chop.

Died as she lived—alone.

How many Grace Llewellen Smiths are there? How many people will die in the loneliness in which they are living? The homeless in Atlanta. The happy-hour hopper in L.A. A bag lady in Miami. The preacher in Nashville. Any person who doubts whether the world needs him. Any person who is convinced that no one really cares.

Any person who has been given a ring, but never a heart; criticism, but never a chance; a bed, but never rest.

These are the victims of futility.

And unless someone intervenes, unless something happens, the epitaph of Grace Smith will be theirs.

That's why the story you are about to read is significant. It's the story of another tombstone. This time, however, the tombstone doesn't mark the death of a person—it marks the birth.[1]

Her eyes squint against the noonday sun. Her shoulders stoop under the weight of the water jar. Her feet trudge, stirring dust on the path. She keeps her eyes down so she can dodge the stares of the others.

She is a Samaritan; she knows the sting of racism. She is a woman; she's bumped her head on the ceiling of sexism. She's been married to five men. Five. Five different marriages. Five different beds. Five different rejections. She knows the sound of slamming doors.

She knows what it means to love and receive no love in return. Her current mate won't even give her his name. He only gives her a place to sleep.

If there is a Grace Llewellen Smith in the New Testament, it is this woman. The epitaph of insignificance could have been hers. And it would have been, except for an encounter with a stranger.

On this particular day, she came to the well at noon. Why hadn't she gone in the early morning with the other women? Maybe she had. Maybe she just needed an extra draw of water on a hot day. Or maybe not. Maybe it was the other women she was avoiding. A walk in the hot sun was a small price to pay in order to escape their sharp tongues.

"Here she comes."

"Have you heard? She's got a new man!"

"They say she'll sleep with anyone."

"Shhh. There she is."

So she came to the well at noon. She expected silence. She expected solitude. Instead, she found one who knew her better than she knew herself.

He was seated on the ground: legs outstretched, hands folded, back resting against the well. His eyes were closed. She stopped and looked at him. She looked around. No one was near. She looked back at him. He was obviously Jewish. What was he doing here? His eyes opened, and hers ducked in embarrassment. She went quickly about her task.

Sensing her discomfort, Jesus asked her for water. But she was too streetwise to think that all he wanted was a drink. "Since when does an uptown fellow like you ask a girl like me for water?" She wanted to know what he really had in mind. Her intuition was partly correct. He was interested in more than water. He was interested in her heart.

They talked. Who could remember the last time a man had spoken to her with respect?

He told her about a spring of water that would quench not the thirst of the throat, but of the soul.

That intrigued her. "Sir, give me this water so that I won't get thirsty and have to keep coming here to draw water."

"Go, call your husband and come back."

Her heart must have sunk. Here was a Jew who didn't care if she was a Samaritan. Here was a man who didn't look down on her as a woman. Here was the closest thing to gentleness she'd ever seen. And now he was asking her about . . . that.

Anything but that. Maybe she considered lying. "Oh, my husband? He's busy." Maybe she wanted to change the subject. Perhaps she wanted to leave—but she stayed. And she told the truth.

"I have no husband." (Kindness has a way of inviting honesty.)

You probably know the rest of the story. I wish you didn't. I wish you were hearing it for the first time. For if you were, you'd be wide-eyed as you waited to see what Jesus would do next. Why? Because you've wanted to do the same thing.

You've wanted to take off your mask. You've wanted to stop pretending. You've wondered what God would do if you opened your cobweb-covered door of secret sin.

This woman wondered what Jesus would do. She must have wondered if the kindness would cease when the truth was revealed. *He will be angry. He will leave. He will think I'm worthless.*

If you've had the same anxieties, then get out your pencil. You'll want to underline Jesus' answer.

"You're right. You have had five husbands, and the man you are with now won't even give you a name."

No criticism? No anger? No what-kind-of-mess-have-you-made-of-your-life lectures?

No. It wasn't perfection that Jesus was seeking; it was honesty.

The woman was amazed.

"I can see that you are a prophet." Translation? "There is something different about you. Do you mind if I ask you something?"

Then she asked the question that revealed the gaping hole in her soul.

"Where is God? My people say he is on the mountain. Your people say he is in Jerusalem. I don't know where he is."

I'd give a thousand sunsets to see the expression on Jesus' face as he heard those words. Did his eyes water? Did he smile? Did he look up into the clouds and wink at his father? Of all the places to find a hungry heart—Samaria?

Of all the Samaritans to be searching for God—a woman?

Of all the women to have an insatiable appetite for God—a five-time divorcée?

And of all the people to be chosen to personally receive the secret of the ages, an outcast among outcasts? The most insignificant person in the region?

Remarkable. Jesus didn't reveal the secret to King Herod. He didn't request an audience of the Sanhedrin and tell them the news. It wasn't within the colonnades of a Roman court that he announced his identity.

No, it was in the shade of a well in a rejected land to an ostracized woman. His eyes must have danced as he whispered the secret.

"I am the Messiah."

The most important phrase in the chapter is one easily overlooked. "Then, leaving her water jar, the woman went back to the town and said to the people, 'Come, see a man who told me everything I ever did. Could this be the Christ?'" (John 4:28–29 NIV).

Don't miss the drama of the moment. Look at her eyes, wide with amazement. Listen to her as she struggles for words. "Y-y-y-you a-a-a-are the M-m-m-messiah!" And watch as she scrambles to her feet, takes one last look at this grinning Nazarene, turns and runs right into the burly chest of Peter. She almost falls, regains her balance, and hotfoots it toward her hometown.

Did you notice what she forgot? She forgot her water jar. She left behind the jug that had caused the sag in her shoulders. She left behind the burden she brought.

Suddenly the shame of the tattered romances disappeared. Suddenly the insignificance of her life was swallowed by the significance of the moment. "God is here! God has come! God cares . . . for me!"

That is why she forgot her water jar. That is why she ran to the city. That is why she grabbed the first person she saw and announced her discovery, "I just talked to a man who knows everything I ever did . . . and he loves me anyway!"

The disciples offered Jesus some food. He refused it—he was too excited! He had just done what he does best. He had taken a life that was drifting and given it direction.

He was exuberant!

"Look!" he announced to disciples, pointing at the woman who was running to the village. "Vast fields of human souls are ripening all around us, and are ready now for the reaping" (John 4:35 TLB).

Who could eat at a time like this?

For some of you the story of these two women is touching but distant. You belong. You are needed and you know it. You've got more friends than you can visit and more tasks than you can accomplish.

Insignificance will not be chiseled on your tombstone.

Be thankful.

But others of you are different. You paused at the epitaph because it was yours. You see the face of Grace Smith when you look into the mirror. You know why the Samaritan woman was avoiding people. You do the same thing.

You know what it's like to have no one sit by you at the cafeteria. You've wondered what it would be like to have one good friend. You've been in love, and you wonder if it is worth the pain to do it again.

And you, too, have wondered where in the world God is.

I have a friend named Joy who teaches underprivileged children in an inner-city church. Her class is a lively group of nine-year-olds who love life and aren't afraid of God. There is one exception, however—a timid girl by the name of Barbara.

Her difficult home life had left her afraid and insecure. For the weeks that my friend was teaching the class, Barbara never spoke. Never. While the other children talked, she sat. While the others sang, she was silent. While the others giggled, she was quiet.

Always present. Always listening. Always speechless.

Until the day Joy gave a class on heaven. Joy talked about seeing God. She talked about tearless eyes and deathless lives.

Barbara was fascinated. She wouldn't release Joy from her stare.

She listened with hunger. Then she raised her hand. "Mrs. Joy?"

Joy was stunned. Barbara had never asked a question. "Yes, Barbara?"

"Is heaven for girls like me?"

Again, I would give a thousand sunsets to have seen Jesus' face as this tiny prayer reached his throne. For indeed that is what it was—a prayer.

An earnest prayer that a good God in heaven would remember a forgotten soul on earth. A prayer that God's grace would seep into the cracks and cover one the church let slip through. A prayer to take a life that no one else could use and use it as no one else could.

Not a prayer from a pulpit, but one from a bed in a convalescent home. Not a prayer prayed confidently by a black-robed seminarian, but one whispered fearfully by a recovering alcoholic.

A prayer to do what God does best: take the common and make it spectacular. To once again take the rod and divide the sea. To take a pebble and kill a Goliath. To take water and make sparkling wine. To take a peasant boy's lunch and feed a multitude. To take mud and restore sight. To take three spikes and a wooden beam and make them the hope of humanity. To take a rejected woman and make her a missionary.

There are two graves in this chapter. The first is the lonely one in the Locke Hill Cemetery. The grave of Grace Llewellen Smith. She knew not love. She knew not gratification. She knew only the pain of the chisel as it carved this epitaph into her life.

> *Sleeps, but rests not.*
> *Loved, but was loved not.*
> *Tried to please, but pleased not.*
> *Died as she lived—alone.*

That, however, is not the only grave in this story. The second is near a water well. The tombstone? A water jug. A forgotten water jug. It has no words, but has great significance—for it is the burial place of insignificance.

· 8 ·

THE VOICE FROM
THE MOP BUCKET

God began doing a good work in you, and I am sure he will
continue it until it is finished when Jesus Christ comes again.

—PHILIPPIANS 1:6

The hallway is silent except for the wheels of the mop bucket and the shuffle of the old man's feet. Both sound tired.

Both know these floors. How many nights has Hank cleaned them? Always careful to get in the corners. Always careful to set up his yellow caution sign warning of wet floors. Always chuckling as he does. "Be careful everyone," he laughs to himself, knowing no one is near.

Not at 3:00 AM.

Hank's health isn't what it used to be. Gout keeps him awake. Arthritis makes him limp. His glasses are so thick his eyeballs look twice their size. Shoulders stoop. But he does his work. Slopping soapy water on linoleum. Scrubbing the heel marks left by the well-heeled lawyers. He'll be finished an hour before quitting time. Always finishes early. Has for twenty years.

When finished he'll put away his bucket and take a seat outside the office of the senior partner and wait. Never leaves early. Could. No one would know. But he doesn't.

He broke the rules once. Never again.

Sometimes, if the door is open, he'll enter the office. Not for long. Just to look. The suite is larger than his apartment. He'll run his finger over the desk. He'll stroke the soft leather couch. He'll stand at the window and watch the gray sky turn gold. And he'll remember.

He once had such an office.

Back when Hank was Henry. Back when the custodian was an executive. Long ago. Before the night shift. Before the mop bucket. Before the maintenance uniform. Before the scandal.

Hank doesn't think about it much now. No reason to. Got in trouble, got fired, and got out. That's it. Not many people know about it. Better that way. No need to tell them.

It's his secret.

Hank's story, by the way, is true. I changed the name and a detail or two. I gave him a different job and put him in a different century. But the story is factual. You've heard it. You know it. When I give you his real name, you'll remember.

But more than a true story, it's a common story. It's a story of a derailed dream. It's a story of high hopes colliding with harsh realities.

Happens to all dreamers. And since all have dreamed, it happens to us all.

In Hank's case, it was a mistake he could never forget. A grave mistake. Hank killed someone. He came upon a thug beating up an innocent man, and Hank lost control. He killed the mugger. When word got out, Hank got out.

Hank would rather hide than go to jail. So he ran. The executive became a fugitive.

True story. Common story. Most stories aren't as extreme as Hank's. Few spend their lives running from the law. Many, however, live with regrets.

"I could have gone to college on a golf scholarship," a fellow told me just last week on the fourth tee box. "Had an offer right out of school. But I joined a rock-and-roll band. Ended up never going. Now I'm stuck fixing garage doors."

"Now I'm stuck." Epitaph of a derailed dream.

Pick up a high school yearbook and read the "What I want to do" sentence under each picture. You'll get dizzy breathing the thin air of mountaintop visions:

"Ivy league school."

"Write books and live in Switzerland."

"Physician in a third-world country."

"Teach inner-city kids."

Yet, take the yearbook to a twentieth-year reunion and read the next chapter. Some dreams have come true, but many haven't. Not that all should, mind you. I hope the little guy who dreamed of being a sumo wrestler came to his senses. And I hope he didn't lose his passion in the process. Changing direction in life is not tragic. Losing passion in life is.

Something happens to us along the way. Convictions to change the world downgrade to commitments to pay the bills. Rather than make a difference, we make a salary. Rather than look forward, we look back. Rather than look outward, we look inward.

And we don't like what we see.

Hank didn't. Hank saw a man who'd settled for the mediocre. Trained in the finest institutions of the world, yet working the night shift in a minimum-wage job so he wouldn't be seen in the day.

But all that changed when he heard the voice from the mop bucket. (Did I mention that his story is true?)

At first he thought the voice was a joke. Some of the fellows on the third floor play these kinds of tricks.

"Henry, Henry," the voice called.

Hank turned. No one called him Henry anymore.

"Henry, Henry."

He turned toward the pail. It was glowing. Bright red. Hot red. He could feel the heat ten feet away. He stepped closer and looked in. The water wasn't boiling.

"This is strange," Hank mumbled to himself as he took another step to get a closer look. But the voice stopped him.

"Don't come any closer. Take off your shoes. You are on holy tile."

Suddenly Hank knew who was speaking. "God?"

I'm not making this up. I know you think I am. Sounds crazy. Almost irreverent. God speaking from a hot mop bucket to a janitor named Hank? Would it be believable if I said God was speaking from a burning bush to a shepherd named Moses?

Maybe that one's easier to handle—because you've heard it before. But just because it's Moses and a bush rather than Hank and a bucket, it's no less spectacular.

It sure shocked the sandals off Moses. We wonder what amazed the old fellow more: that God spoke in a bush or that God spoke at all.

Moses, like Hank, had made a mistake.

You remember his story. Adopted nobility. An Israelite reared in an Egyptian palace. His countrymen were slaves, but Moses was privileged. Ate at the royal table. Educated in the finest schools.

But his most influential teacher had no degree. She was his mother. A Jewess who was hired to be his nanny. "Moses," you can almost hear her whisper to her young son, "God has put you here on purpose. Someday you will set your people free. Never forget, Moses. Never forget."

Moses didn't. The flame of justice grew hotter until it blazed. Moses saw an Egyptian beating a Hebrew slave. Just as Hank killed the mugger, Moses killed the Egyptian.

The next day Moses saw the Hebrew. You'd think the slave would say thanks. He didn't. Rather than express gratitude, he expressed anger. "Will you kill me too?" he asked (see Exod. 2:14).

Moses knew he was in trouble. He fled Egypt and hid in the wilderness. Call it a career shift. He went from dining with the heads of state to counting heads of sheep.

Hardly an upward move.

And so it happened that a bright, promising Hebrew began herding sheep in the hills. From the Ivy League to the cotton patch. From the Oval Office to a taxicab. From swinging a golf club to digging a ditch.

Moses thought the move was permanent. There is no indication he ever intended to go back to Egypt. In fact, there is every indication he wanted to stay with his sheep. Standing barefoot before the bush, he confessed, "I am not a great man! How can I go to the king and lead the Israelites out of Egypt?" (Exod. 3:11).

I'm glad Moses asked that question. It's a good one. Why Moses? Or, more specifically, why eighty-year-old Moses?

The forty-year-old version was more appealing. The Moses we saw in Egypt was brash and confident. But the Moses we find four decades later is reluctant and weather-beaten.

Had you and I looked at Moses back in Egypt, we would have said, "This man is ready for battle." Educated in the finest system in the world. Trained by the ablest soldiers. Instant access to the inner circle of the Pharaoh. Moses spoke their language and knew their habits. He was the perfect man for the job.

Moses at forty we like. But Moses at eighty? No way. Too old. Too tired. Smells like a shepherd. Speaks like a foreigner. What impact would he have on Pharaoh? He's the wrong man for the job.

And Moses would have agreed. "Tried that once before," he would say. "Those people don't want to be helped. Just leave me here to tend my sheep. They're easier to lead."

Moses wouldn't have gone. You wouldn't have sent him. I wouldn't have sent him.

But God did. How do you figure? Benched at forty and suited up at eighty. Why? What does he know now that he didn't know then? What did he learn in the desert that he didn't learn in Egypt?

The ways of the desert, for one. Forty-year-old Moses was a city boy. Octogenarian Moses knows the name of every snake and the location of every watering hole. If he's going to lead thousands of Hebrews into the wilderness, he better know the basics of Desert Life 101.

Family dynamics, for another. If he's going to be traveling with families for forty years, it might help to understand how they work. He marries a woman of faith, the daughter of a Midianite priest, and establishes his own family.

But more than the ways of the desert and the people, Moses needed to learn something about himself.

Apparently he has learned it. God says Moses is ready.

And to convince him, God speaks through a bush. (Had to do something dramatic to get Moses' attention.)

"School's out," God tells him. "Now it's time to get to work." Poor Moses. He didn't even know he was enrolled.

But he was. And, guess what. So are you. The voice from the bush is the voice that whispers to you. It reminds you that God is not finished with you yet. Oh, you may think he is. You may think you've peaked. You may think he's got someone else to do the job.

If so, think again.

"God began doing a good work in you, and I am sure he will continue it until it is finished when Jesus Christ comes again" (Phil. 1:6).

Did you see what God is doing? *A good work in you.*

Did you see when he will be finished? *When Jesus comes again.*

May I spell out the message? *God ain't finished with you yet.*

Your Father wants you to know that. And to convince you, he may surprise you. He may speak through a bush, a mop bucket, or stranger still, he may speak through this book.

· 9 ·

GUILT OR GRACE

We have freedom now, because Christ made us free. So
stand strong.

—GALATIANS 5:1

There is an old story about the time Emperor Frederick the Great visited Potsdam Prison. He spoke with the prisoners, and each man claimed to be innocent, a victim of the system. One man, however, sat silently in the corner.

The ruler asked him, "And you, sir, who do you blame for your sentence?"

His response was, "Your majesty, I am guilty and richly deserve my punishment." Surprised, the emperor shouted for the prison warden: "Come and get this man out of here before he corrupts all these innocent people."[1]

The ruler can set us free once we admit we are wrong.

We do ourselves no favors in justifying our deeds or glossing over our sins. When my daughter Andrea was five or six, she got a splinter in her finger. I took her to the restroom and set out some tweezers, ointment, and a Band-Aid.

She didn't like what she saw. "I just want the Band-Aid, Daddy."

Sometimes we are just like Andrea. We come to Christ with our sin, but all we want is a covering. We want to skip the treatment. We want to hide our sin. And one wonders if God, even in his great mercy, will heal what we conceal. "If we say we have no sin, we are fooling ourselves, and the truth is not in us. But if we confess our sins, he will forgive our sins, because we can trust God to do what is right" (1 John 1:8–9).

Going to God is not going to Santa Claus. A child sits on the chubby lap of Ol' Saint Nick, and Santa pinches the youngster's cheek and asks, "Have you been a good little girl?"

"Yes," she giggles. Then she tells him what she wants and down she bounds. It's a game. It's childish. No one takes Santa's question seriously. That may work in a department store, but it won't work with God.

How can God heal what we deny? How can God touch what we cover up? How can we have communion while we keep secrets? How can God grant us pardon when we won't admit our guilt?

Ahh, there's that word: *guilt*. Isn't that what we avoid? Guilt. Isn't that what we detest? But is guilt so bad? What does guilt imply if not that we know right from wrong, that we aspire to be better than we are, that we know there is a high country and we are in the low country. That's what guilt is: a healthy regret for telling God one thing and doing another.

Guilt is the nerve ending of the heart. It yanks us back when we are too near the fire. Godly sorrow "makes people change their hearts and lives. This leads to salvation, and you cannot be sorry for that" (2 Cor. 7:10).

To feel guilt is no tragedy; to feel no guilt is.

· 10 ·

THE ELEVENTH HOUR GIFT

*There were also two criminals led out with Jesus to be put
to death. When they came to a place called the Skull, the
soldiers crucified Jesus and the criminals—one on his right
and the other on his left. Jesus said, "Father, forgive them,
because they don't know what they are doing."*

*The soldiers threw lots to decide who would get his
clothes. The people stood there watching. And the leaders
made fun of Jesus, saying, "He saved others. Let him save
himself if he is God's Chosen One, the Christ."*

*The soldiers also made fun of him, coming to Jesus and
offering him some vinegar. They said, "If you are the king
of the Jews, save yourself!" At the top of the cross these words
were written:* THIS IS THE KING OF THE JEWS.

*One of the criminals on a cross began to shout insults
at Jesus: "Aren't you the Christ? Then save yourself and us."*

*But the other criminal stopped him and said, "You
should fear God! You are getting the same punishment
he is. We are punished justly, getting what we deserve for
what we did. But this man has done nothing wrong." Then*

*he said, "Jesus, remember me when you come into your
kingdom."*

*Jesus said to him, "I tell you the truth, today you will
be with me in paradise."*

—LUKE 23:32-43

The educated. The powerful. The rejected. The sick. The lonely. The wealthy. Who would have ever assembled such a crew? All they had in common were their empty hope chests, long left vacant by charlatans and profiteers. Though they had nothing to offer, they asked for everything: a new birth, a second chance, a fresh start, a clean conscience. And without exception their requests were honored.

And now, one more beggar comes with a request. Only minutes from the death of them both, he stands before the King. He will ask for crumbs. And he, like the others, will receive a whole loaf.

Skull's hill—windswept and stony. The thief—gaunt and pale.

Hinges squeak as the door of death closes on his life.

His situation is pitiful. He's taking the last step down the spiral staircase of failure. One crime after another. One rejection after another. Lower and lower he descended until he reached the bottom—a crossbeam and three spikes.

He can't hide who he is. His only clothing is the cloak of his disgrace. No fancy jargon. No impressive résumé. No Sunday school awards. Just a naked history of failure.

He sees Jesus.

Earlier he had mocked the man. When the crowd first chorused its criticism, he'd sung his part (Matt. 27:44). But now he doesn't mock Jesus. He studies him. He begins to wonder who this man might be.

How strange. He doesn't resist the nails; he almost invites them.

He hears the jests and the insults and sees the man remain quiet. He sees the fresh blood on Jesus' cheeks, the crown of thorns scraping Jesus' scalp, and he hears the hoarse whisper, "Father, forgive them."

Why do they want him dead?

Slowly the thief's curiosity offsets the pain in his body. He momentarily forgets the nails rubbing against the raw bones of his wrists and the cramps in his calves.

He begins to feel a peculiar warmth in his heart: he begins to care; he begins to care about this peaceful martyr.

There's no anger in his eyes, only tears.

He looks at the huddle of soldiers throwing dice in the dirt, gambling for a ragged robe. He sees the sign above Jesus' head. It's painted with sarcasm: King of the Jews.

They mock him as a king. If he were crazy, they would ignore him. If he had no followers, they'd turn him away. If he were nothing to fear, they wouldn't kill him. You only kill a king if he has a kingdom.

Could it be . . .

His cracked lips open to speak.

Then, all of a sudden, his thoughts are exploded by the accusations of the criminal on the other cross. He, too, has been studying Jesus, but studying through the blurred lens of cynicism.

"So you're the Messiah, are you? Prove it by saving yourself—and us, too, while you're at it!" (Luke 23:39 TLB).

It's an inexplicable dilemma—how two people can hear the same words and see the same Savior, and one see hope and the other see nothing but himself.

It was all the first criminal could take. Perhaps the crook who hurled the barb expected the other crook to take the cue and hurl a few of his own. But he didn't. No second verse was sung. What the bitter-tongued criminal did hear were words of defense.

"Don't you fear God?"

Only minutes before these same lips had cursed Jesus. Now they are defending him. Every head on the hill lifts to look at this one who spoke on behalf of the Christ. Every angel weeps and every demon gapes.

Who could have imagined this thief thinking of anyone but himself? He'd always been the bully, the purse-snatching brat. Who could remember the last time he'd come to someone's aid? But as the last grains of sand trickle through his hourglass, he performs man's noblest act. He speaks on God's behalf.

Where are those we would expect to defend Jesus?

A much more spiritual Peter has abandoned him.

A much more educated Pilate has washed his hands of him.

A much more loyal mob of countrymen has demanded his death.

A much more faithful band of disciples has scattered.

When it seems that everyone has turned away, a crook places himself between Jesus and the accusers and speaks on his behalf.

"Don't you even fear God when you are dying? We deserve to die for our evil deeds, but this man hasn't done one thing wrong" (Luke 23:40 TLB).

The soldiers look up. The priests cease chattering. Mary wipes her tears and raises her eyes. No one had even noticed the fellow, but now everyone looks at him.

Perhaps even Jesus looks at him. Perhaps he turns to see the one who had spoken when all others had remained silent. Perhaps he fights to focus his eyes on the one who offered this final gesture of love he'd receive while alive. I wonder, did he smile as this sheep straggled into the fold?

For that, in effect, is exactly what the criminal is doing. He is stumbling to safety just as the gate is closing. Lodged in the thief's statement are the two facts that anyone needs to recognize in order to come to Jesus. Look at the phrase again. Do you see them?

"We are getting what we deserve. This man has done nothing wrong" (Luke 23:41 TLB).

We are guilty and he is innocent.

We are filthy and he is pure.

We are wrong and he is right.

He is not on that cross for his sins. He is there for ours.

And once the crook understands this, his request seems only natural. As he looks into the eyes of his last hope, he made the same request any Christian has made.

"Remember me when you come into your kingdom" (Luke 23:42).

No stained-glass homilies. No excuses. Just a desperate plea for help.

At this point Jesus performs the greatest miracle of the cross. Greater than the earthquake. Greater than the tearing of the temple curtain. Greater than the darkness. Greater than the resurrected saints appearing on the streets.

He performs the miracle of forgiveness. A sin-soaked criminal is received by a blood-stained Savior.

"Today you will be with me in Paradise. This is a solemn promise" (Luke 23:43 TLB).

Wow. Only seconds before the thief was a beggar nervously squeezing his hat at the castle door, wondering if the King might spare a few crumbs. Suddenly he's holding the whole pantry.

Such is the definition of grace.

· II ·

IMPERFECT PEOPLE

Come to me, all of you who are tired and have heavy loads, and I will give you rest. Accept my teachings and learn from me, because I am gentle and humble in spirit, and you will find rest for your lives. The burden that I ask you to accept is easy; the load I give you to carry is light.

—MATTHEW 11:28-30

The woman flops down on the bench and drops her trash bag between her feet. With elbows on knees and cheeks in hands, she stares at the sidewalk. Everything aches. Back. Legs. Neck. Her shoulder is stiff and her hands raw. All because of the sack.

Oh, to be rid of this garbage.

Unbroken clouds form a gray ceiling, gray with a thousand sorrows. Soot-stained buildings cast long shadows, darkening passageways and the people in them. Drizzle chills the air and muddies the rivulets of the street gutters. The woman collects her jacket. A passing car drenches the sack and splashes her jeans. She doesn't move. Too tired.

Her memories of life without the trash are fuzzy. As a child maybe? Her back was straighter, her walk quicker . . . or was it a dream? She doesn't know for sure.

A second car. This one stops and parks. A man steps out. She watches his shoes sink in the slush. From the car he pulls out a trash bag, lumpy with litter. He drapes it over his shoulder and curses the weight.

Neither of them speaks. Who knows if he noticed her. His face seems young, younger than his stooped back. In moments he is gone. Her gaze returns to the pavement.

She never looks at her trash. Early on she did. But what she saw repulsed her, so she's kept the sack closed ever since.

What else can she do? Give it to someone? All have their own.

Here comes a young mother. With one hand she leads a child; with the other she drags her load, bumpy and heavy.

Here comes an old man, face ravined with wrinkles. His trash sack is so long it hits the back of his legs as he walks. He glances at the woman and tries to smile.

What weight would he be carrying? she wonders as he passes.

"Regrets."

She turns to see who spoke. Beside her on the bench sits a man. Tall, with angular cheeks and bright, kind eyes. Like hers, his jeans are mud stained. Unlike hers, his shoulders are straight. He wears a T-shirt and baseball cap. She looks around for his trash but doesn't see it.

He watches the old man disappear as he explains, "As a young father, he worked many hours and neglected his family. His children don't love him. His sack is full, full of regrets."

She doesn't respond. And when she doesn't, he does.

"And yours?"

"Mine?" she asks, looking at him.

"Shame." His voice is gentle, compassionate.

She still doesn't speak, but neither does she turn away.

"Too many hours in the wrong arms. Last year. Last night . . . shame."

She stiffens, steeling herself against the scorn she has learned to expect. As if she needed more shame. Stop him. But how? She awaits his judgment.

But it never comes. His voice is warm and his question honest. "Will you give me your trash?"

Her head draws back. *What can he mean?*

"Give it to me. Tomorrow. At the landfill. Will you bring it?" He rubs a moist smudge from her cheek with his thumb and stands. "Friday. The landfill."

Long after he leaves, she sits, replaying the scene, retouching her cheek. His voice lingers; his invitation hovers. She tries to dismiss his words but can't. How could he know what he knew? And how could he know and still be so kind? The memory sits on the couch of her soul, an uninvited but welcome guest.

That night's sleep brings her summer dreams. A young girl under blue skies and puffy clouds, playing amid wildflowers, skirt twirling. She dreams of running with hands wide open, brushing the tops of sunflowers. She dreams of happy people filling a meadow with laughter and hope.

But when she wakes, the sky is dark, the clouds billowed, and the streets shadowed. At the foot of her bed lies her sack of trash. Hoisting it over her shoulder, she walks out of the apartment and down the stairs and onto the street, still slushy.

It's Friday.

For a time she stands, thinking. First wondering what he meant, then if he really meant it. She sighs. With hope just barely outweighing hopelessness, she turns toward the edge of town. Others are walking in the same direction. The man beside her smells of alcohol. He's slept many nights in his suit. A teenage girl walks a few feet ahead. The woman of shame hurries to catch up. The girl volunteers an answer before the question can be asked: "Rage. Rage at my father. Rage at my mother. I'm tired of anger. He said he'd take it." She motions to the sack. "I'm going to give it to him."

The woman nods, and the two walk together.

The landfill is tall with trash—papers and broken brooms and old beds and rusty cars. By the time they reach the hill, the line to the top is long. Hundreds walk ahead of them. All wait in silence, stunned by what they hear—a scream, a pain-pierced roar that hangs in the air for moments, interrupted only by a groan. Then the scream again.

His.

As they draw nearer, they know why. He kneels before each, gesturing toward the sack, offering a request, then a prayer. "May I have it? And may you never feel it again." Then he bows his head and lifts the sack, emptying its contents upon himself. The selfishness of the glutton, the bitterness of the angry, the possessiveness of the insecure. He feels what they felt. It is as if he'd lied or cheated or cursed his Maker.

Upon her turn, the woman pauses. Hesitates. His eyes compel her to step forward. He reaches for her trash and takes it from her. "You can't live with this," he explains. "You weren't made to." With head down, he empties her shame upon his shoulders. Then looking toward the heavens with tear-flooded eyes, he screams, "I'm sorry!"

"But you did nothing!" she cries.

Still, he sobs as she has sobbed into her pillow a hundred nights. That's when she realizes that his cry is hers. Her shame his.

With her thumb she touches his cheek, and for the first step in a long nighttime, she has no trash to carry.

With the others she stands at the base of the hill and watches as he is buried under a mound of misery. For some time he moans. Then nothing. Just silence.

The people sit among the wrecked cars and papers and discarded stoves and wonder who this man is and what he has done. Like mourners at a wake, they linger. Some share stories. Others say nothing. All cast occasional glances at the landfill. It feels odd, loitering near the heap. But it feels even stranger to think of leaving.

So they stay. Through the night and into the next day. Darkness comes again. A kinship connects them, a kinship through the trashman. Some doze. Others build fires in the metal drums and speak of the sudden abundance of stars in the night sky. By early morning most are asleep.

They almost miss the moment. It is the young girl who sees it. The girl with the rage. She doesn't trust her eyes at first, but when she looks again, she knows.

Her words are soft, intended for no one. "He's standing."

Then aloud, for her friend, "He's standing."

And louder for all, "He's standing!"

She turns; all turn. They see him silhouetted against a golden sun.

Standing. Indeed.

... FOR THE
PRIDEFUL

Humble yourself in the Lord's presence,
and he will honor you.

—JAMES 4:10

· 12 ·

THE KINGDOM OF THE ABSURD

If anyone thinks he has a reason to trust in himself, he should know that I have greater reason for trusting in myself. I was circumcised eight days after my birth. I am from the people of Israel and the tribe of Benjamin. I am a Hebrew, and my parents were Hebrews. I had a strict view of the law, which is why I became a Pharisee. I was so enthusiastic I tried to hurt the church. No one could find fault with the way I obeyed the law of Moses. Those things were important to me, but now I think they are worth nothing because of Christ. Not only those things, but I think that all things are worth nothing compared with the greatness of knowing Christ Jesus my Lord.

—PHILIPPIANS 3:4-8

My power shows up best in weak people" (2 Cor. 12:9 TLB). God said those words. Paul wrote them down. God said he was looking for empty vessels more than strong muscles. Paul proved it.

Before he encountered Christ, Paul had been somewhat of a hero among the Pharisees. You might say he was their Wyatt Earp. He kept the law and order—or, better said, revered the Law and gave the orders. Good Jewish moms held him up as an example of a good Jewish boy. He was given the seat of honor at the Jerusalem Lions Club Wednesday luncheon. He had a "Who's Who in Judaism" paperweight on his desk and was selected "Most Likely to Succeed" by his graduating class. He was quickly establishing himself as the heir apparent to his teacher, Gamaliel.

If there is such a thing as a religious fortune, Paul had it. He was a spiritual billionaire, born with one foot in heaven, and he knew it:

> If anyone ever had reason to hope that he could save himself, it would be I. If others could be saved by what they are, certainly I could! For I went through the Jewish initiation ceremony when I was eight days old, having been born into a pure-blooded Jewish home that was a branch of the old original Benjamin family. So I was a real Jew if there ever was one! What's more, I was a member of the Pharisees who demand the strictest obedience to every Jewish law and custom. And sincere? Yes, so much so that I greatly persecuted the Church; and I tried to obey every Jewish rule and regulation down to the very last point. (Phil. 3:4–6 TLB)

Blue-blooded and wild-eyed, this young zealot was hell-bent on keeping the kingdom pure—and that meant keeping the Christians out. He marched through the countryside like a general demanding that backslidden Jews salute the flag of the motherland or kiss their family and hopes good-bye.

All this came to a halt, however, on the shoulder of a highway. Equipped with subpoenas, handcuffs, and a posse, Paul was on his way to do a little personal evangelism in Damascus. That's when someone slammed on the stadium lights, and he heard the voice.

When he found out whose voice it was, his jaw hit the ground, and his body followed. He braced himself for the worst. He knew it was all over. He felt the noose around his neck. He smelled the flowers in the hearse. He prayed that death would be quick and painless.

But all he got was silence and the first of a lifetime of surprises.

He ended up bewildered and befuddled in a borrowed bedroom. God left him there a few days with scales on his eyes so thick that the only direction he could look was inside himself. And he didn't like what he saw.

He saw himself for what he really was—to use his own words, the worst of sinners (1 Tim. 1:15). A legalist. A killjoy. A bumptious braggart who claimed to have mastered God's code. A dispenser of justice who weighed salvation on a panscale.

That's when Ananias found him. He wasn't much to look at—haggard and groggy after three days of turmoil. Sarai wasn't much to look at either, nor was Peter. But what the three have in common says more than a volume of systematic theology. For when they gave up, God stepped in, and the result was a roller-coaster ride straight into the kingdom.

Paul was a step ahead of the rich young ruler. He knew better than to strike a deal with God. He didn't make any excuses; he just pleaded for mercy. Alone in the room with his sins on his conscience and blood on his hands, he asked to be cleansed.

Ananias's instructions to Paul are worth reading: "What are you waiting for? Get up, be baptized and wash your sins away, calling on his name" (Acts 22:16 NIV).

He didn't have to be told twice. The legalist Saul was buried, and the liberator Paul was born. He was never the same afterward. And neither was the world.

Stirring sermons, dedicated disciples, and six thousand miles of trails. If his sandals weren't slapping, his pen was writing. If he wasn't explaining the mystery of grace, he was articulating the theology that would determine the course of Western civilization.

All of his words could be reduced to one sentence. "We preach Christ crucified" (1 Cor. 1:23 NIV). It wasn't that he lacked other sermon outlines; it was just that he couldn't exhaust the first one.

The absurdity of the whole thing kept him going. Jesus should have finished him on the road. He should have left him for the buzzards. He should have sent him to hell. But he didn't. He sent him to the lost.

Paul himself called it crazy. He described it with phrases like "stumbling block" and "foolishness," but chose in the end to call it "grace" (1 Cor. 1:23; Eph. 2:8 NIV).

And he defended his unquenchable loyalty by saying, "The love of Christ leaves [me] no choice" (1 Cor. 5:14 NEB).

Paul never took a course in missions. He never sat in on a committee meeting. He never read a book on church growth. He was just inspired by the Holy Spirit and punch-drunk on the love that makes the impossible possible: salvation.

The message is gripping: Show a man his failures without Jesus, and the result will be found in the roadside gutter. Give a man religion without reminding him of his filth, and the result will be arrogance in a three-piece suit. But get the two in the same heart—get sin to meet Savior and Savior to meet sin—and the result just might be another Pharisee turned preacher who sets the world on fire.

· 13 ·

DRESSED IN HIS RIGHTEOUSNESS ALONE

You were all baptized into Christ, and so you were all
clothed with Christ. This means that you are all children of
God through faith in Christ Jesus.

—GALATIANS 3:26-27

For years I owned an elegant suit complete with coat, trousers, even a hat. I considered myself quite dapper in the outfit and was confident others agreed.

The pants were cut from the cloth of my good works, sturdy fabric of deeds done and projects completed. Some studies here, some sermons there. Many people complimented my trousers, and I confess, I tended to hitch them up in public so people would notice them.

The coat was equally impressive. It was woven together

from my convictions. Each day I dressed myself in deep feelings of religious fervor. My emotions were quite strong. So strong, in fact, that I was often asked to model my cloak of zeal in public gatherings to inspire others. Of course I was happy to comply.

While there I'd also display my hat, a feathered cap of knowledge. Formed with my own hands from the fabric of personal opinion, I wore it proudly.

Surely God is impressed with my garments, I often thought. Occasionally I strutted into his presence so he could compliment the self-tailored wear. He never spoke. *His silence must mean admiration,* I convinced myself.

But then my wardrobe began to suffer. The fabric of my trousers grew thin. My best works started coming unstitched. I began leaving more undone than done, and what little I did was nothing to boast about.

No problem, I thought. *I'll work harder.*

But working harder *was* a problem. There was a hole in my coat of convictions. My resolve was threadbare. A cold wind cut into my chest. I reached up to pull my hat down firmly, and the brim ripped off in my hands.

Over a period of a few months, my wardrobe of self-righteousness completely unraveled. I went from tailored gentlemen's apparel to beggars' rags. Fearful that God might be angry at my tattered suit, I did my best to stitch it together and cover my mistakes. But the cloth was so worn. And the wind was so icy. I gave up. I went back to God. (Where else could I go?)

On a wintry Thursday afternoon, I stepped into his presence, not for applause, but for warmth. My prayer was feeble.

"I feel naked."

"You are. And you have been for a long time."

What he did next I'll never forget. "I have something to give you," he said. He gently removed the remaining threads and then picked up a robe, a regal robe, the clothing of his own goodness. He wrapped it around my shoulders. His words to me were tender. "My son, you are now clothed with Christ" (see Gal. 3:27).

Though I'd sung the hymn a thousand times, I finally understood it:

Dressed in his righteousness alone,
faultless to stand before the throne.[1]

· 14 ·

WHERE MAN COVERS
HIS MOUTH

Then Job answered the LORD:
> *"I know that you can do all things*
>> *and that no plan of yours can be ruined.*
> *You asked, 'Who is this that made my purpose unclear by*
>> *saying things that are not true?'*
>> *Surely I spoke of things I did not understand;*
>> *I talked of things too wonderful for me to know.*
> *You said, 'Listen now, and I will speak.*
>> *I will ask you questions,*
>> *and you must answer me.'*
> *My ears had heard of you before,*
>> *but now my eyes have seen you."*

—JOB 42:1–5

There are times when to speak is to violate the moment . . . when silence represents the highest respect.

This was a lesson Job learned. If he had a fault, it was his tongue. He talked too much.

Not that anyone could blame him. Calamity had pounced on the man like a lioness on a herd of gazelles, and by the time the rampage passed, there was hardly a wall standing or a loved one living. Enemies had slaughtered Job's cattle, and lightning had destroyed his sheep. Strong winds had left his partying kids buried in wreckage.

And that was just the first day.

Job hadn't even had time to call Allstate before he saw the leprosy on his hands and the boils on his skin. His wife, compassionate soul that she was, told him to "curse God and die." His four friends came with the bedside manner of drill sergeants, telling him that God is fair and pain is the result of evil, and as sure as two-plus-two equals four, Job must have some criminal record in his past to suffer so.

Each had his own interpretation of God and each spoke long and loud about who God is and why God did what he did. They weren't the only ones talking about God. When his accusers paused, Job gave his response. Back and forth they went . . .

Job cried out . . . (3:1).

Then Eliphaz the Temanite answered . . . (4:1).

Then Job answered . . . (6:1).

Then Bildad the Shuhite answered . . . (8:1).

Then Job answered . . . (9:1).

98

Then Zophar the Naamathite answered . . . (11:1).

This verbal ping-pong continues for twenty-three chapters. Finally Job has enough of this "answering." No more discussion-group chit-chat. It's time for the keynote address. He grips the microphone with one hand and the pulpit with the other and launches forth. For six chapters Job gives his opinions on God. This time the chapter headings read: "And Job continued," "And Job continued," "And Job continued." He defines God, explains God, and reviews God. One gets the impression that Job knows more about God than God does!

We are thirty-seven chapters into the book before God clears his throat to speak. Chapter thirty-eight begins with these words: "Then the LORD answered Job."

If your Bible is like mine, there is a mistake in this verse. The words are fine but the printer uses the wrong size type. The words should look like this:

THEN THE LORD ANSWERED JOB!

God speaks. Faces turn toward the sky. Winds bend the trees. Neighbors plunge into the storm shelters. Cats scurry up the trees, and dogs duck into the bushes. "Somethin's a-blowin' in, honey. Best get them sheets off the line." God has no more than opened his mouth before Job knows he should have kept his sore one shut.

> I will ask you questions
> and you must answer me.
> Where were you when I made the earth's foundation?

Tell me, if you understand.
Who marked off how big it should be? Surely you know!
Who stretched a ruler across it?
What were the earth's foundations set on,
or who put its cornerstone in place
while the morning stars sang together
and all the angels shouted with joy? (38:3–7)

God floods the sky with queries, and Job cannot help but get the point: only God defines God. You've got to know the alphabet before you can read, and God tells Job, "You don't even know the ABC's of heaven, much less the vocabulary." For the first time, Job is quiet. Silenced by a torrent of questions.

Have you ever gone to where the sea begins
or walked the valleys under the sea? . . .
Have you ever gone to the storehouse for snow
or seen the storehouses for hail . . . ?
Are you the one who gives the horse his strength
or puts the flowing mane on its neck?
Do you make the horse jump like a locust . . . ?
Is it through your wisdom that the hawk flies
and spreads its wings toward the south?
(38:16, 22; 39:19–20, 26)

Job barely has time to shake his head at one question before he is asked another. The Father's implication is clear: "As soon as you are able to handle these simple matters of storing stars and stretching the neck of the ostrich, then we'll have a talk about pain and suffering. But until then, we can do without your commentary."

Does Job get the message? I think so. Listen to his response. "I am not worthy; I cannot answer you anything, / so I will put my hand over my mouth" (40:4).

Notice the change. Before he heard God, Job couldn't speak enough. After he heard God, he couldn't speak at all.

Silence was the only proper response. There was a time in the life of Thomas à Kempis when he, too, covered his mouth. He had written profusely about the character of God. But one day God confronted him with such holy grace that, from that moment on, all à Kempis's words "seemed like straw." He put down his pen and never wrote another line. He put his hand over his mouth.

The word for such moments is reverence.

· 15 ·

TANK YOUR REPUTATION

*But [Jesus] gave up his place with God and made himself
nothing.*

  *He was born as a man
  and became like a servant.*

*And when he was living as a man,
  he humbled himself and was fully obedient to God,
  even when that caused his death—death on a cross.*

—PHILIPPIANS 2:7-8

My teenage acquaintances included a handful of
Christians, none of whom were cool. One minister's
daughter passed on beer parties and gossip. As a result, she spent
most lunch hours and Friday nights alone. A tennis player came
back from summer break with a Bible bumper sticker on his car
and a smile on his face. We called him a Jesus freak.

My voice was among the mockers. It shouldn't have been,

but it was. Somewhere inside I knew better, but I didn't go there for advice. My parents took me to church. My minister told me about Christ. But did I make a big deal about God or the church? No. I had something far more important to promote.

My reputation. An athlete, a flirt, a beer drinker, a partyer. I polished and protected my reputation like a '65 Mustang. What mattered most to me was people's opinion of me.

But then I went off to college and heard a professor describe a Christ I'd never seen. A people-loving and death-defeating Christ. A Jesus who made time for the lonely, the losers . . . a Jesus who died for hypocrites like me. So I signed up. As much as I could, I gave him my heart.

Not long after that decision, I traveled home to meet some of the old gang. Only minutes into the trip I grew nervous. My friends didn't know about my faith. I wasn't sure I wanted them to. I remembered the jokes we had told about the preacher's daughter and the Jesus freak. Did I dare risk hearing the same said about me? Didn't I have my status to protect?

One can't, at once, promote two reputations. Promote God's and forget yours. Or promote yours and forget God's. We must choose.

Joseph did. Matthew describes Jesus's earthly father as a craftsman (Matt. 13:55). He lives in Nazareth: a single-camel map dot on the edge of boredom. Joseph never speaks in the New Testament. He *does* much. He sees an angel, marries a pregnant girl, and leads his family to Bethlehem and Egypt. He does much, but says nothing.

A small-town carpenter who never said a Scripture-worthy

word. Is Joseph the right choice? Doesn't God have better options? An eloquent priest from Jerusalem or a scholar from the Pharisees? Why Joseph? A major part of the answer lies in his reputation: he gives it up for Jesus. "Then Joseph [Mary's] husband, being a just man, and not wanting to make her a public example, was minded to put her away secretly" (Matt. 1:19 NKJV).

With the phrase "a just man," Matthew recognizes the status of Joseph. He was a *tsadiq* (tsa-DEEK), a serious student of the Torah.[1] Nazareth viewed Joseph as we might view an elder, deacon, or Bible class teacher. *Tsadiqs* studied God's law. They recited and lived the *Shema*[2] daily. They supported the synagogue, observed holy days, and followed the food restrictions. For a common carpenter to be known as a *tsadiq* was no small thing. Joseph likely took pride in his standing, but Mary's announcement jeopardized it. *I'm pregnant.*

Mary's parents, by this point, have signed a contract and sealed it with a dowry. Mary belongs to Joseph; Joseph belongs to Mary. Legally and matrimonially bound.

Now what? What's a *tsadiq* to do? His fiancée is pregnant, blemished, tainted . . . he is righteous, godly. On one hand, he has the law. On the other, he has his love. The law says, stone her. Love says, forgive her. Joseph is caught in the middle. But Joseph is a kind man. "Not wanting to disgrace her, [he] planned to send her away secretly" (v. 19 NASB).

A quiet divorce. How long would it stay quiet? Likely not long. But for a time, this was the solution.

Then comes the angel. "While he thought about these things, behold, an angel of the Lord appeared to him in a dream, saying, 'Joseph, son of David, do not be afraid to take to you Mary your wife, for that which is conceived in her is of the Holy Spirit'" (v. 20 NKJV).

Mary's growing belly gives no cause for concern, but reason to rejoice. "She carries the Son of God in her womb," the angel announces. But who would believe it? Who would buy this tale? Envision Joseph being questioned by the city leaders.

"Joseph," they say, "we understand that Mary is with child."

He nods.

"Is the child yours?"

He shakes his head.

"Do you know how she became pregnant?"

Gulp. A bead of sweat forms beneath Joseph's beard. He faces a dilemma. Make up a lie and preserve his place in the community, or tell the truth and kiss his *tsadiq* good-bye. He makes his decision. "Joseph . . . took to him his wife, and did not know her till she had brought forth her firstborn Son. And he called His name JESUS" (Matt. 1:24–25 NKJV).

Joseph tanked his reputation. He swapped his *tsadiq* diploma for a pregnant fiancée and an illegitimate son and made the big decision of discipleship. He placed God's plan ahead of his own.

Would you be willing to do the same? God grants us an uncommon life to the degree we surrender our common one. "If you try to keep your life for yourself, you will lose it. But if you give up your life for me, you will find true life" (Matt. 16:25 NLT). Would you forfeit your reputation to see Jesus born into your world?

Consider these situations:

You're a photographer for an ad agency. Your boss wants to assign you to your biggest photo shoot ever. The account? An adult magazine. He knows of your faith. Say yes and polish your reputation. Say yes and use your God-given gift to tarnish Christ's reputation. What do you choose?

The college philosophy teacher daily harangues against Christ. He derides spirituality and denigrates the need for forgiveness. One day he dares any Christian in the class to speak up. Would you?

One more. You enjoy the role of a Christmas Christian. You sing the carols, attend the services . . . Come January, you'll jettison your faith and reshelve your Bible. But during December, you soar.

But this December something hits you. The immensity of it all hits you. *Heaven hung her highest hope and King on a cross, for me.* Radical thoughts begin to surface: joining a weekly Bible study, going on a mission trip, volunteering at a soup kitchen. Your family and friends think you are crazy. Your changing world changes theirs. They want the Christmas Christian back.

You can protect your reputation or protect his. You have a choice.

Joseph made his.

Jesus did too. He "made Himself of no reputation, taking the form of a bondservant, and coming in the likeness of men. And being found in appearance as a man, He humbled Himself and became obedient to the point of death, even the death of the cross" (Phil. 2:7–8 NKJV).

Christ abandoned his reputation. No one in Nazareth saluted him as the Son of God. He did not stand out in his elementary-classroom photograph, demanded no glossy page in his high school annual. Friends knew him as a woodworker, not a star hanger. His looks turned no heads; his position earned him no credit. In the great stoop we call Christmas, Jesus abandoned heavenly privileges and aproned earthly pains. "He gave up his place with God and made himself nothing" (Phil. 2:7).

God hunts for those who will do likewise—Josephs through whom he can deliver Christ into the world.

Deflating inflated egos is so important to God that he offers to help.

He helped me. I recently spent an autumn week on a book tour. We saw long lines and crowded stores. One person after another complimented me. For three days I bathed in the river of praise. I began to believe the accolades. *All these people can't be wrong. I must be God's gift to readers.* My chest puffed so much I could hardly see where to autograph the books. Why, had I been born two thousand years earlier, we might read the gospels of Matthew, *Max*, Luke, and John. About the time I wondered if the Bible needed another epistle, God shot an arrow of humility in my direction.

We were running late for an evening book signing, late because the afternoon signing had seen such long lines. We expected the same at the next store. Concerned, we phoned ahead. "We are running behind. Tell all the people we'll arrive soon."

"No need to hurry," the store manager assured.

"What about the people?"

"Neither one seems to be in a hurry."

Neither one?

By the time we reached the store, thankfully, the crowd of two people had tripled to six. We had scheduled two hours for the signing; I needed ten minutes.

Self-conscious about sitting alone at the table, I peppered the last person with questions. We talked about her parents, school, Social Security number, favorite birthday party. Against my pleadings, she had to go. So I sat alone at the table. Big stack of Lucado books, no one in line.

I asked the store manager, "Did you advertise?"

"We did. More than usual." She walked off.

The next time she passed I asked, "Had other signings?"

"Yes, usually we have a great response," and kept going.

I signed all the books at my table. I signed all the Lucado books on the shelves. I signed Tom Clancy and John Grisham books. Finally a customer came to the table. "You write books?" he asked, picking up the new one.

"I do. Want me to sign it?"

"No thanks," he answered and left.

God hit his target. Lest I forget, my daily reading the next morning had this passage: "Do not be wise in your own eyes" (Prov. 3:7 NKJV).

When you're full of yourself, God can't fill you.

But when you empty yourself, God has a useful vessel. Your Bible overflows with examples of those who did.

In his gospel, Matthew mentions his own name only twice.

Both times he calls himself a tax collector. In his list of apostles, he assigns himself the eighth spot.

John doesn't even mention his name in his gospel. The twenty appearances of "John" all refer to the Baptist. John the apostle simply calls himself the "other disciple" or the "disciple whom Jesus loved."

Luke wrote two of the most important books in the Bible but never once penned his own name.

Paul, the Bible's most prolific author, referred to himself as "a fool" (2 Cor. 12:11). He also called himself "the least of the apostles" (1 Cor. 15:9 NKJV). Five years later he claimed to be "less than the least of all the saints" (Eph. 3:8 NKJV). In one of his final epistles he referred to himself as the "chief" of sinners (1 Tim. 1:15 NKJV). As he grew older, his ego grew smaller.

King David wrote no psalm celebrating his victory over Goliath. But he wrote a public poem of penitence confessing his sin with Bathsheba (see Ps. 51).

And then there is Joseph. The quiet father of Jesus. Rather than make a name for himself, he made a home for Christ. And because he did, a great reward came his way. "He called His name JESUS" (Matt. 1:25 NKJV).

Queue up the millions who have spoken the name of Jesus, and look at the person selected to stand at the front of the line. Joseph. Of all the saints, sinners, prodigals, and preachers who have spoken the name, Joseph, a blue-collar, small-town construction worker, said it first. He cradled the wrinkle-faced Prince of Heaven and, with an audience of angels and pigs, whispered, "Jesus . . . You'll be called Jesus."

Seems right, don't you think? Joseph gave up his name. So Jesus let Joseph say his. You think Joseph regretted his choice?

I didn't regret mine. I went to the hometown party. As expected, everyone asked questions like, "What's the latest?" I told them. Not gracefully or eloquently . . . but honestly. "My faith," I remember saying. "I'm taking faith real seriously."

A few rolled their eyes. Others made mental notes to remove my name from their party list. But one or two found their way over and confided, "I've been thinking the same thing."

Turns out I wasn't standing alone after all.

. . . FOR THE
MISTAKE-MAKERS

*If we confess our sins, he will forgive our sins,
because we can trust God to do what is right. He
will cleanse us from all the wrongs we have done.*

—1 JOHN 1:9

· 16 ·

THE TENDERNESS OF GOD

*For our high priest is able to understand our weaknesses. He
was tempted in every way that we are, but he did not sin.
Let us, then, feel very sure that we can come before God's
throne where there is grace. There we can receive mercy and
grace to help us when we need it.*

—HEBREWS 4:15-16

When my daughter Jenna was eight, she sang a solo at an appreciation banquet. I agreed to stay home with our other two daughters if my wife would film the performance. When they came home, they had quite a story to tell and quite a tape to show.

Jenna forgot her lines. As she stood onstage in front of a large audience, her mind went blank. Since Denalyn was filming the moment, I saw the crisis through her eyes, the eyes of a mom. You can tell Denalyn is getting nervous the minute Jenna is getting forgetful—the camera begins to shake. "It's okay, it's okay," Denalyn's voice assures. She begins singing the words so Jenna will remember. But it's too late. Jenna says "I'm sorry" to the audience, bursts into tears, and bolts off the stage.

At this point Mom drops the camera and runs after Jenna. The camera records the floor and Denalyn's voice saying, "Come here, honey."

Why did Denalyn do that? Why did she drop everything and run after her daughter? (By the way, Jenna recovered. Denalyn dried her tears. The two rehearsed the lyrics. And Jenna sang and received a loud ovation.)

Now, why did Denalyn go to all that trouble? In the great scheme of things, does a social embarrassment matter that much? You know the answer before I tell you. To an eight-year-old girl, it's crucial. And because it was important to Jenna, it was important to Mom.

And because you are God's child, if it's important to you, it's important to God.

· 17 ·

PUPPIES, BUTTERFLIES, AND A SAVIOR

What a miserable man I am! Who will save me from this body that brings me death? I thank God for saving me through Jesus Christ our Lord!

—ROMANS 7:24-25

When I was ten years old, I had a puppy named Tina. You would have loved her. She was the perfect pet. An irresistible, pug-nosed Pekingese pup. One ear fell over, and the other ear stood straight up. She never tired of playing and yet never got in the way.

Her mother died when she was born so the rearing of the puppy fell to me. I fed her milk from a doll bottle and used to sneak out at night to see if she was warm. I'll never forget the night I took her to bed with me only to have her mess on my pillow. We made quite a pair. My first brush with parenthood.

One day I went into the backyard to give Tina her dinner. I looked around and spotted her in a corner near the fence. She had cornered a butterfly (as much as a butterfly can be cornered) and was playfully yelping and jumping in the air trying to catch the butterfly in her mouth. Amused, I watched her for a few minutes and then called to her.

"Tina! Come here, girl! It's time to eat!"

What happened next surprised me. Tina stopped her playing and looked at me. But instead of immediately scampering in my direction, she sat back on her haunches.

Then she tilted her head back toward the butterfly, looked back at me, then back to the butterfly, and then back to me. For the first time in her life, she had to make a decision.

Her "want to" longed to pursue the butterfly which tauntingly awaited her in midair. Her "should" knew she was supposed to obey her master. A classic struggle of the will: a war between the "want" and the "should." The same question that has faced every adult now faced my little puppy.

And do you know what she did? She chased the butterfly! Scurrying and barking, she ignored my call and chased that silly thing until it flew over the fence.

That is when the guilt hit.

She stopped at the fence for a long time, sitting back on her hind legs looking up in the air where the butterfly had made its exit. Slowly, the excitement of the chase was overshadowed by the guilt of disobedience.

She turned painfully and walked back to encounter her owner. (To be honest, I was a little miffed.) Her head was ducked as she regretfully trudged across the yard.

For the first time in her life, she felt guilty.

She had violated her "should" and had given in to her "want." My heart melted, however, and I called her name again. Sensing forgiveness, Tina darted into my hands. (I always was a softy.)

Now, I may be overdoing it a bit. I don't know if a dog can really feel guilty or not. But I do know a human can. And whether the sin is as slight as chasing a butterfly or as serious as sleeping with another man's wife, the effects are the same.

Guilt creeps in on cat's paws and steals whatever joy might have flickered in our eyes. Confidence is replaced by doubt, and honesty is elbowed out by rationalization. Exit peace. Enter turmoil. Just as the pleasure of indulgence ceases, the hunger for relief begins.

Our vision is shortsighted, and our myopic life now has but one purpose—to find release for our guilt. Or as Paul questioned for all of us, "What a wretched man I am! Who will rescue me from this body of death?" (Rom. 7:24 NIV).

That's not a new question. One hardly opens the Bible before he encounters humanity coping, or more frequently, failing to cope, with guilt. Adam and Eve's rebellion led to shame and hiding. Cain's jealousy led to murder and banishment. And before long, the entire human race was afflicted. Evil abounded and the people grew wicked. The heart of man grew so cold that he no longer sought relief for his callused conscience. And, in what has to be the most fearful Scripture in the Bible, God says that he was sorry that he had made man on earth (Gen. 6:6).

All of this from man's inability to cope with sin.

If only we had a guilt-kidney that would pass on our failures or a built-in eraser that would help us live with ourselves. But we don't. In fact, that is precisely the problem.

Man cannot cope with guilt alone.

When Adam was created, he was created without the ability to cope with guilt. Why? Because he was not made to make mistakes. But when he did, he had no way to deal with it. When God pursued him to help him, Adam covered his nakedness and hid in shame.

Man by himself cannot deal with his own guilt. He must have help from the outside. In order to forgive himself, he must have forgiveness from the one he has offended. Yet man is unworthy to ask God for forgiveness.

That, then, is the whole reason for the cross.

The cross did what sacrificed lambs could not do. It erased our sins, not for a year, but for eternity. The cross did what man could not do. It granted us the right to talk with, love, and even live with God.

You can't do that by yourself. I don't care how many worship services you attend or good deeds you do, your goodness is insufficient. You *can't* be good enough to deserve forgiveness. No one bats a thousand. No one bowls three hundred. No one. Not you, not me, not anyone.

That's why we have guilt in the world.

That's why we need a savior.

You can't forgive me for my sins nor can I forgive you for yours. Two kids in a mud puddle can't clean each other. They need someone clean. Someone spotless. We need someone clean too.

That's why we need a Savior.

What my little puppy needed was exactly what you and I need—a master who would extend his hands and say, "Come on, that's okay." We don't need a master who will judge us on our performance, or we'll fall woefully short. Trying to make it to heaven on our own goodness is like trying to get to the moon on a moon beam; nice idea, but try it and see what happens.

Listen. Quit trying to quench your own guilt. You can't do it. There's no way. Not with a bottle of whiskey or perfect Sunday school attendance. Sorry. I don't care how bad you are. You can't be bad enough to forget it. And I don't care how good you are. You can't be good enough to overcome it.

You need a Savior.

· 18 ·

NOT GUILTY

The teachers of the law and the Pharisees brought a woman who had been caught in adultery. They forced her to stand before the people. They said to Jesus, "Teacher, this woman was caught having sexual relations with a man who is not her husband. The law of Moses commands that we stone to death every woman who does this. What do you say we should do?" They were asking this to trick Jesus so that they could have some charge against him.

But Jesus bent over and started writing on the ground with his finger. When they continued to ask Jesus their question, he raised up and said, "Anyone here who has never sinned can throw the first stone at her." Then Jesus bent over again and wrote on the ground.

Those who heard Jesus began to leave one by one, first the older men and then the others. Jesus was left there alone with the woman standing before him. Jesus raised up again and asked her, "Woman, where are they? Has no one judged you guilty?"

She answered, "No one, sir."

Then Jesus said, "I also don't judge you guilty. You
may go now, but don't sin anymore."

—JOHN 8:3-11

That's her, the woman standing in the center of the circle. Those men around her are religious leaders. Pharisees, they are called. Self-appointed custodians of conduct. And the other man, the one in the simple clothes, the one sitting on the ground, the one looking at the face of the woman, that's Jesus.

Jesus has been teaching.

The woman has been cheating.

And the Pharisees are out to stop them both.

"Teacher, this woman was caught in the act of adultery" (John 8:4 NIV). The accusation rings off the courtyard walls.

"Caught in the act of adultery." The words alone are enough to make you blush. Doors slammed open. Covers jerked back.

"In the act." In the arms. In the moment. In the embrace.

"Caught." Aha! What have we here? This man is not your husband. Put on some clothes! We know what to do with women like you!

In an instant she is yanked from private passion to public spectacle. Heads poke out of windows as the posse pushes her through the streets. Dogs bark. Neighbors turn. The city sees. Clutching a thin robe around her shoulders, she hides her nakedness.

But nothing can hide her shame.

From this second on, she'll be known as an adulteress. When she goes to the market, women will whisper. When she passes, heads will turn. When her name is mentioned, the people will remember.

Moral failure finds easy recall.

The greater travesty, however, goes unnoticed. What the woman did is shameful, but what the Pharisees did is despicable. According to the law, adultery was punishable by death, but only if two people witnessed the act. There had to be two eyewitnesses.

Question: How likely are two people to be eyewitnesses to adultery? What are the chances of two people stumbling upon an early morning flurry of forbidden embraces? Unlikely. But if you do, odds are it's not a coincidence.

So we wonder. How long did the men peer through the window before they barged in? How long did they lurk behind the curtain before they stepped out?

And what of the man? Adultery requires two participants. What happened to him? Could it be that he slipped out?

The evidence leaves little doubt. It was a trap. She's been caught. But she'll soon see that she is not the catch—she's only the bait.

"The law of Moses commands that we stone to death every woman who does this. What do you say we should do?" (v. 5).

Pretty cocky, this committee of high ethics. Pretty proud of themselves, these agents of righteousness. This will be a moment they long remember, the morning they foil and snag the mighty Nazarene.

As for the woman? Why, she's immaterial. Merely a pawn in their game. Her future? It's unimportant. Her reputation? Who cares if it's ruined? She is a necessary, yet dispensable, part of their plan.

The woman stares at the ground. Her sweaty hair dangles. Her tears drip hot with hurt. Her lips are tight; her jaw is clenched. She knows she's been framed. No need to look up. She'll find no kindness. She looks at the stones in their hands. Squeezed so tightly that fingertips turn white.

She thinks of running. But where? She could claim mistreatment. But to whom? She could deny the act, but she was seen. She could beg for mercy, but these men offer none.

The woman has nowhere to turn.

You'd expect Jesus to stand and proclaim judgment on the hypocrites. He doesn't. You'd hope that he would snatch the woman and the two would be beamed to Galilee. That's not what happens either. You'd imagine that an angel would descend or heaven would speak or the earth would shake. No, none of that.

Once again, his move is subtle.

But, once again, his message is unmistakable.

What does Jesus do? (If you already know, pretend you don't and feel the surprise.)

Jesus writes in the sand.

He stoops down and draws in the dirt. The same finger that engraved the commandments on Sinai's peak and seared the warning on Belshazzar's wall now scribbles in the courtyard floor. And as he writes, he speaks: "Anyone here who has never sinned can throw the first stone at her" (v. 7).

The young look to the old. The old look in their hearts. They are the first to drop their stones. And as they turn to leave, the young who were cocky with borrowed convictions do the same. The only sound is the thud of rocks and the shuffle of feet.

Jesus and the woman are left alone. With the jury gone, the courtroom becomes the judge's chambers, and the woman awaits his verdict. *Surely, a sermon is brewing. No doubt, he's going to demand that I apologize.* But the judge doesn't speak. His head is down, perhaps he's still writing in the sand. He seems surprised when he realizes that she is still there.

"Woman, where are they? Has no one judged you guilty?"

She answers, "No one, sir."

Then Jesus says, "I also don't judge you guilty. You may go now, but don't sin anymore" (vv. 10–11).

If you have ever wondered how God reacts when you fail, frame these words and hang them on the wall. Read them. Ponder them. Drink from them. Stand below them and let them wash over your soul.

· 19 ·

THE RING OF BELIEF

My dear brothers and sisters, always be willing to listen and
slow to speak.

—JAMES 1:19

You don't have to speak to encourage. The Bible says, "It is best to listen much, speak little" (James 1:19 TLB). We tend to speak much and listen little. There is a time to speak. But there is also a time to be quiet. That's what my father did. Dropping a fly ball may not be a big deal to most people, but if you are thirteen years old and have aspirations of the big leagues, it is a big deal. Not only was it my second error of the game, it allowed the winning run to score.

I didn't even go back to the dugout. I turned around in the middle of left field and climbed over the fence. I was halfway home when my dad found me. He didn't say a word. Just pulled over to the side of the road, leaned across the seat, and opened the passenger door. We didn't speak. We didn't need to. We both knew the world had come to an end. When we got home, I went straight to my room, and he went straight to the kitchen. Presently he appeared in front of me with cookies and milk. He took a seat on the bed, and we broke bread together. Somewhere in the dunking of the cookies I began to realize that life and my father's love would go on. In the economy of male adolescence, if you love the guy who drops the ball, then you really love him. My skill as a baseball player didn't improve, but my confidence in Dad's love did. Dad never said a word. But he did show up. He did listen up. That's what your Father God does. His presence may be quiet, but he'll show up. And he'll listen.

· 20 ·

WHEN GRACE GOES DEEP

For we are God's masterpiece. He has created us anew in
Christ Jesus, so we can do the good things he planned for us
long ago.

—EPHESIANS 2:10 NLT

O ver a hundred years ago, a group of fishermen were
relaxing in the dining room of a Scottish seaside inn,
trading fish stories. One of the men gestured widely, depict-
ing the size of a fish that got away. His arm struck the serving
maid's tea tray, sending the teapot flying into the whitewashed
wall, where its contents left an irregular brown splotch.

The innkeeper surveyed the damage and sighed, "The
whole wall will have to be repainted."

"Perhaps not," offered a stranger. "Let me work with it."

Having nothing to lose, the proprietor consented. The man
pulled pencils, brushes, some jars of linseed oil, and pigment out

of an art box. He sketched lines around the stains and dabbed shades and colors throughout the splashes of tea. In time, an image began to emerge: a stag with a great rack of antlers. The man inscribed his signature at the bottom, paid for his meal, and left. His name: Sir Edwin Landseer, famous painter of wildlife.

In his hands, a mistake became a masterpiece.[1]

God's hands do the same, over and over. He draws together the disjointed blotches in our life and renders them an expression of his love. We become pictures, "examples of the incredible wealth of his favor and kindness toward us" (Eph. 2:7 NLT).

Receive God's work. Drink deeply from his well of grace.

· 21 ·

WHAT WE REALLY
WANT TO KNOW

*Who can accuse the people God has chosen? No one, because
God is the One who makes them right. Who can say God's
people are guilty? No one, because Christ Jesus died, but he
was also raised from the dead, and now he is on God's right
side, appealing to God for us.*

—ROMANS 8:33–34

Sometime ago I read a story of a youngster who was shoot-
ing rocks with a slingshot. He could never hit his target. As
he returned to Grandma's backyard, he spied her pet duck. On
impulse he took aim and let fly. The stone hit, and the duck was
dead. The boy panicked and hid the bird in the woodpile, only
to look up and see his sister watching.

After lunch that day, Grandma told Sally to help with the

dishes. Sally responded, "Johnny told me he wanted to help in the kitchen today. Didn't you Johnny?" And she whispered to him, "Remember the duck!" So, Johnny did the dishes.

What choice did he have? For the next several weeks he was at the sink often. Sometimes for his duty, sometimes for his sin. "Remember the duck," Sally'd whisper when he objected.

So weary of the chore, he decided that any punishment would be better than washing more dishes, so he confessed to killing the duck. "I know, Johnny," his grandma said, giving him a hug. "I was standing at the window and saw the whole thing. Because I love you, I forgave you. I wondered how long you would let Sally make a slave out of you."[1]

. . . FOR A
FALTERING FAITH

I tell you the truth, you can say to this mountain,
"Go, fall into the sea." And if you have no
doubts in your mind and believe that what
you say will happen, God will do it for you.

—MARK 11:23

· 22 ·

THE GOSPEL OF THE SECOND CHANCE

When the Sabbath was over, Mary Magdalene, Mary the mother of James, and Salome bought spices so that they might go to anoint Jesus' body. Very early on the first day of the week, just after sunrise, they were on their way to the tomb and they asked each other, "Who will roll the stone away from the entrance of the tomb?"

But when they looked up, they saw that the stone, which was very large, had been rolled away. As they entered the tomb, they saw a young man dressed in a white robe sitting on the right side, and they were alarmed.

"Don't be alarmed," he said. "You are looking for Jesus the Nazarene, who was crucified. He has risen! He is not here. See the place where they laid him. But go, tell his disciples and Peter, 'He is going ahead of you into Galilee. There you will see him, just as he told you.'"

—MARK 16:1-7 NIV

I t was like discovering the prize in a box of Cracker Jacks or spotting a little pearl in a box of buttons or stumbling across a ten dollar bill in a drawer full of envelopes.

It was small enough to overlook. Only two words. I know I'd read that passage a hundred times. But I'd never seen it. Maybe I'd passed over it in the excitement of the resurrection. Or, since Mark's account of the resurrection is by far the briefest of the four, maybe I'd just not paid too much attention. Or, maybe since it's in the last chapter of the gospel, my weary eyes had always read too quickly to note this little phrase.

But I won't miss it again. It's highlighted in yellow and underlined in red. You might want to do the same. Look in Mark, chapter 16. Read the first five verses about the women's surprise when they find the stone moved to the side. Then feast on that beautiful phrase spoken by the angel, "He is not here, he is risen," but don't pause for too long. Go a bit further. Get your pencil ready and enjoy this jewel in the seventh verse (here it comes). The verse reads something like this: "But go, tell his disciples and Peter that he is going before you to Galilee."

Did you see it? Read it again. (This time I italicized the words.)

"But go, tell his disciples *and Peter* that he is going before you to Galilee."

Now tell me if that's not a hidden treasure.

If I might paraphrase the words, "Don't stay here, go tell the disciples," a pause, then a smile, "and especially tell Peter, that he is going before you to Galilee."

What a line. It's as if all of heaven had watched Peter fall—and it's as if all of heaven wanted to help him back up again. "Be sure and tell Peter that he's not left out. Tell him that one failure doesn't make a flop."

Whew!

No wonder they call it the gospel of the second chance.

Not many second chances exist in the world today. Just ask the kid who didn't make the little league team or the fellow who got the pink slip or the mother of three who got dumped for a "pretty little thing."

Not many second chances. Nowadays it's more like, "It's now or never." "Around here we don't tolerate incompetence." "Gotta get tough to get along." "Not much room at the top." "Three strikes and you're out." "It's a dog-eat-dog world!"

Jesus has a simple answer to our masochistic mania. "It's a dog-eat-dog world?" he would say. "Then don't live with the dogs." That makes sense doesn't it? Why let a bunch of other failures tell you how much of a failure you are?

Sure you can have a second chance.

Just ask Peter. One minute he felt lower than a snake's belly, and the next minute he was the high hog at the trough. Even the angels wanted this distraught netcaster to know that it wasn't over. The message came loud and clear from the celestial Throne Room through the divine courier. "Be sure and tell Peter that he gets to bat again."

Those who know these types of things say that the Gospel of Mark is really the transcribed notes and dictated thoughts of Peter. If this is true, then it was Peter himself who included these two words! And if these really are his words, I can't help but imagine that the old fisherman had to brush away a tear and swallow a lump when he got to this point in the story.

It's not every day that you get a second chance. Peter must have known that. The next time he saw Jesus, he got so excited that he barely got his britches on before he jumped into the cold water of the Sea of Galilee. It was also enough, so they say, to cause this backwoods Galilean to carry the gospel of the second chance all the way to Rome where they killed him. If you've ever wondered what would cause a man to be willing to be crucified upside down, maybe now you know.

It's not every day that you find someone who will give you a second chance—much less someone who will give you a second chance every day.

But in Jesus, Peter found both.

· 23 ·

REMEMBER

When it was evening on the first day of the week, Jesus'
followers were together. The doors were locked, because they
were afraid of the elders. Then Jesus came and stood right
in the middle of them and said, "Peace be with you."

—JOHN 20:19

The church of Jesus Christ began with a group of frightened men in a second-floor room in Jerusalem.

Though trained and taught, they didn't know what to say. Though they'd marched with him for three years, they now sat . . . afraid. They were timid soldiers, reluctant warriors, speechless messengers.

Their most courageous act was to get up and lock the door.

Some looked out the window, some looked at the wall, some looked at the floor, but all looked inside themselves.

And well they should, for it was an hour of self-examination.

All their efforts seemed so futile. Nagging their memories were the promises they'd made but not kept. When the Roman soldiers took Jesus, Jesus' followers took off. With the very wine of the covenant on their breath and the bread of his sacrifice in their bellies, they fled.

All those boasts of bravado? All those declarations of devotion? They lay broken and shattered at the gate of Gethsemane's garden.

We don't know where the disciples went when they fled the garden, but we do know what they took: a memory. They took a heart-stopping memory of a man who called himself no less than God in the flesh. And they couldn't get him out of their minds. Try as they might to lose him in the crowd, they couldn't forget him. If they saw a leper, they thought of his compassion. If they heard a storm, they would remember the day he silenced one. If they saw a child, they would think of the day he held one. And if they saw a lamb being carried to the temple, they would remember his face streaked with blood and his eyes flooded with love.

No, they couldn't forget him. As a result, they came back. And, as a result, the church of our Lord began with a group of frightened men in an upper room.

Sound familiar? Things haven't changed much in two thousand years, have they? How many churches today find themselves paralyzed in the upper room?

How many congregations have just enough religion to come together, but not enough passion to go out? If the doors aren't locked, they might as well be.

Upper-room futility. A little bit of faith but very little fire.

"Sure, we're doing our part to reach the world. Why, just last year we mailed ten correspondence courses. We're anticipating a response any day now."

"You bet we care that the world is reached! We send $150 a month to . . . uh, well . . . ol' what's-his-name down there in . . . uh, well, oh, I forget the place, but . . . we pray for it often."

"World hunger? Why, that's high on our priority list! In fact, we have plans to plan a planning session. At least, that is what we are planning to do."

Good people. Lots of ideas. Plenty of good intentions. Budgets. Meetings. Words. Promises. But while all this is going on, the door remains locked and the story stays a secret.

You don't turn your back on Christ, but you don't turn toward him either. You don't curse his name, but neither do you praise it. You know you should do something, but you're not sure what. You know you should come together, but you're not sure why.

Upper-room futility. Confused ambassadors behind locked doors. What will it take to unlock them? What will it take to ignite the fire? What will it take to restore the first-century passion? What will have to happen before the padlocks of futility tumble from our doors and are trampled under the feet of departing disciples?

More training? That's part of it. Better strategies? That would help. A greater world vision? Undoubtedly. More money? That's imperative. A greater dependence on the Holy Spirit? Absolutely.

But in the midst of these items there is one basic ingredient that cannot be overlooked. There is one element so vital that its absence ensures our failure. What is needed to get us out is exactly what got the apostles out.

Picture the scene. Peter, John, James. They came back. Banking on some zany possibility that the well of forgiveness still had a few drops, they came back. Daring to dream that the master had left them some word, some plan, some direction, they came back.

But little did they know their wildest dream wasn't wild enough. Just as someone mumbles, "It's no use," they hear a noise. They hear a voice.

"Peace be with you" (John 20:19).

Every head lifted. Every eye turned. Every mouth dropped open. Someone looked at the door.

It was still locked.

It was a moment the apostles would never forget, a story they would never cease to tell. The stone of the tomb was not enough to keep him in. The walls of the room were not enough to keep him out.

The one betrayed sought his betrayers. What did he say to them? Not "What a bunch of flops!" Not "I told you so." No "Where-were-you-when-I-needed-you?" speeches. But simply one phrase, "Peace be with you." The very thing they didn't have was the very thing he offered: peace.

It was too good to be true! So amazing was the appearance that some were saying, "Pinch me, I'm dreaming" even at the ascension (Matt. 28:17; author's paraphrase). No wonder they returned to Jerusalem with great joy! (Luke 24:52). No wonder they were always in the temple praising God! (Luke 24:53).

A transformed group stood beside a transformed Peter as he announced some weeks later, "Therefore let all Israel be assured of this: God has made this Jesus, whom you crucified, both Lord and Christ" (Acts 2:36 NIV).

No timidity in his words. No reluctance. About three thousand people believed his message.

The apostles sparked a movement. The people became followers of the death-conqueror. They couldn't hear enough or say enough about him. People began to call them "Christ-ians." Christ was their model, their message. They preached "Jesus Christ and him crucified," not for the lack of another topic, but because they couldn't exhaust this one.

What unlocked the doors of the apostles' hearts?

Simple. They saw Jesus. They encountered the Christ. Their sins collided with their Savior, and their Savior won! What lit the boiler of the apostles was a red-hot conviction that the very one who should have sent them to hell, went to hell for them and came back to tell about it.

A lot of things would happen to them over the next few decades. Many nights would be spent away from home. Hunger would gnaw at their bellies. Rain would soak their skin. Stones would bruise their bodies. Shipwrecks, lashings, martyrdom. But there was a scene in the repertoire of memories that caused them never to look back: the betrayed coming back to find his betrayers, not to scourge them, but to send them. Not to criticize them for forgetting, but to commission them to remember.

Remember that he who was dead is alive and they who were guilty have been forgiven.

Think about the first time you ever saw him. Think about your first encounter with the Christ. Robe yourself in that moment. Resurrect the relief. Recall the purity. Summon forth the passion. Can you remember?

I can. 1965. A red-headed ten-year-old with a tornado of freckles sits in a Bible class on a Wednesday night. What I remember of the class are scenes—school desks with initials carved in them. A blackboard. A dozen or so kids, some listening, some not. A teacher wearing a suit coat too tight to button around his robust belly.

He is talking about Jesus. He is explaining the cross. I know I had heard it before, but that night I heard it for sure. "You can't save yourself; you need a savior." I can't explain why it connected that night as opposed to another, but it did. He simply articulated what I was beginning to understand—I was lost— and he explained what I needed—a redeemer. From that night on, my heart belonged to Jesus.

Many would argue that a ten-year-old is too young for such a decision. And they may be right. All I know is that I never made a more earnest decision in my life. I didn't know much about God, but what I knew was enough. I knew I wanted to go to heaven. And I knew I couldn't do it alone.

No one had to tell me to be happy. No one had to tell me to tell others. They couldn't keep me quiet. I told all my friends at school. I put a bumper sticker on my bicycle. And though I'd never read 2 Corinthians 4:13, I knew what it meant. "I believed; therefore I have spoken" (NIV). Pardon truly received is pardon powerfully proclaimed.

There is a direct correlation between the accuracy of our memories and the effectiveness of our missions. If we are not teaching people how to be saved, it is perhaps because we have forgotten the tragedy of being lost! If we're not teaching the message of forgiveness, it may be because we don't remember what it was like to be guilty. And if we're not preaching the cross, it could be that we've subconsciously decided that—God forbid—somehow we don't need it.

In what was perhaps the last letter Paul ever wrote, he begged Timothy not to forget. In a letter written within earshot of the sharpening of the blade that would sever his head, he urged Timothy to remember. "Remember Jesus Christ. . . ." (2 Tim. 2:8 NIV). You can almost picture the old warrior smiling as he wrote the words. "Remember Jesus Christ, raised from the dead, descended from David. This is my gospel . . ."

When times get hard, remember Jesus. When people don't listen, remember Jesus. When tears come, remember Jesus. When disappointment is your bed partner, remember Jesus. When fear pitches his tent in your front yard. When death looms, when anger singes, when shame weighs heavily. Remember Jesus.

Remember holiness in tandem with humanity. Remember the sick who were healed with callused hands. Remember the dead called from the grave with a Galilean accent. Remember the eyes of God that wept human tears. And, most of all, remember this descendant of David who beat the hell out of death.

Can you still remember? Are you still in love with him?

Remember, Paul begged, remember Jesus. Before you remember anything, remember him. If you forget anything, don't forget him.

Oh, but how quickly we forget. So much happens through the years. So many changes within. So many alterations without. And, somewhere, back there, we leave him. We don't turn away from him . . . we just don't take him with us. Assignments come. Promotions come. Budgets are made. Kids are born, and the Christ . . . the Christ is forgotten.

Has it been a while since you stared at the heavens in speechless amazement? Has it been a while since you realized God's divinity and your carnality?

If it has, then you need to know something. He is still there. He hasn't left. Under all those papers and books and reports and years. In the midst of all those voices and faces and memories and pictures, he is still there.

Do yourself a favor. Stand before him again. Or, better, allow him to stand before you. Go into your upper room and wait. Wait until he comes. And when he appears, don't leave. Run your fingers over his feet. Place your hand in the pierced side. And look into those eyes. Those same eyes that melted the gates of hell and sent the demons scurrying and Satan running. Look at them as they look at you. You'll never be the same.

A man is never the same after he simultaneously sees his utter despair and Christ's unbending grace. To see the despair without the grace is suicidal. To see the grace without the despair is upper-room futility. But to see them both is conversion.

· 24 ·

LEAVE ROOM FOR THE MAGIC

Thomas (called Didymus), who was one of the twelve, was not with them when Jesus came. The other followers kept telling Thomas, "We saw the Lord."

But Thomas said, "I will not believe it until I see the nail marks in his hands and put my finger where the nails were and put my hand into his side."

A week later the followers were in the house again, and Thomas was with them. The doors were locked, but Jesus came in and stood right in the middle of them. He said, "Peace be with you." Then he said to Thomas, "Put your finger here, and look at my hands. Put your hand here in my side. Stop being an unbeliever and believe."

Thomas said to him, "My Lord and my God!"

—JOHN 20:24-28

Thomas. He defies tidy summary.

Oh, I know we've labeled him. Somewhere in some sermon somebody called him "Doubting Thomas." And the nickname stuck. And it's true, he *did* doubt. It's just that there was more to it than that. There was more to his questioning than a simple lack of faith. It was more due to a lack of imagination. You see it in more than just the resurrection story.

Consider, for instance, the time that Jesus was talking in all eloquence about the home he was going to prepare. Though the imagery wasn't easy for Thomas to grasp, he was doing his best. You can see his eyes filling his face as he tries to envision a big white house on St. Thomas Avenue. And just when Thomas is about to get the picture, Jesus assumes, "You know the way that I am going." Thomas blinks a time or two, looks around at the other blank faces, and then bursts out with candid aplomb, "Lord, we don't know where you are going, so how can we know the way?" (John 14:5 NIV). Thomas didn't mind speaking his mind. If you don't understand something, say so! His imagination would only stretch so far.

And then there was the time that Jesus told his disciples he was going to go be with Lazarus even though Lazarus was already dead and buried. Thomas couldn't imagine what Jesus was referring to, but if Jesus was wanting to go back into the arena with those Jews who had tried once before to stone him, Thomas wasn't going to let him face them alone. So he patted his trusty sidearm and said, "Let's die with him!" (John 11:16; author's paraphrase). Thomas had spent his life waiting on the Messiah, and now that the Messiah was here, Thomas was willing to spend his life for him. Not much imagination, but a lot of loyalty.

Perhaps it is this trait of loyalty that explains why Thomas wasn't in the Upper Room when Jesus appeared to the other apostles. You see, I think Thomas took the death of Jesus pretty hard. Even though he couldn't quite comprehend all the metaphors that Jesus at times employed, he was still willing to go to the end with him. But he had never expected that the end would come so abruptly and prematurely. As a result, Thomas was left with a crossword puzzle full of unanswered riddles.

On the one hand, the idea of a resurrected Jesus was too farfetched for dogmatic Thomas. His limited creativity left little room for magic or razzle dazzle. Besides, he wasn't about to set himself up to be disappointed again. One disappointment was enough, thank you. Yet, on the other hand, his loyalty made him yearn to believe. As long as there was the slimmest thread of hope, he wanted to be counted in.

His turmoil, then, came from a fusion between his lack of imagination and his unwavering loyalty. He was too honest with life to be gullible and yet was too loyal to Jesus to be unfaithful. In the end, it was this realistic devotion that caused him to utter the now famous condition, "Unless I see the nail marks in his hands and put my fingers where the nails were, I will not believe it" (John 20:25; author's paraphrase).

So, I guess you could say that he did doubt. But it was a different kind of doubting that springs not from timidity or mistrust, but from a reluctance to believe the impossible and a simple fear of being hurt twice.

Most of us are the same way, aren't we? In our world of budgets, long-range planning, and computers, don't we find it hard to trust in the unbelievable? Don't most of us tend to scrutinize life behind furrowed brows and walk with cautious steps? It's hard for us to imagine that God can surprise us. To make a little room for miracles today, well, it's not sound thinking.

As a result, we, like Thomas, find it hard to believe that God can do the very thing that he is best at: replacing death with life. Our infertile imaginations bear little hope that the improbable will occur. We then, like Thomas, let our dreams fall victim to doubt.

We make the same mistake that Thomas made: we forget that *impossible* is one of God's favorite words.

How about you? How is your imagination these days? When was the last time you let some of your dreams elbow out your logic? When was the last time you imagined the unimaginable? When was the last time you dreamed of an entire world united in peace or all believers united in fellowship? When was the last time you dared dream of the day when every mouth will be fed and every nation dwell in peace? When was the last time you dreamed about every creature on earth hearing about the Messiah? Has it been awhile since you claimed God's promise to do "more than all we ask or imagine?" (Eph. 3:20 NIV).

Though it went against every logical bone in his body, Thomas said he would believe if he could have just a little proof. And Jesus (who is ever so patient with our doubting) gave Thomas exactly what he requested. He extended his hands one more time. And was Thomas ever surprised. He did a double take, fell flat on his face, and cried, "My Lord and my God!" (John 20:28 NIV).

Jesus must have smiled.

He knew he had a winner in Thomas. Anytime you mix loyalty with a little imagination, you've got a man of God on your hands. A man who will die for a truth. Just look at Thomas. Legend has him hopping a freighter to India where they had to kill him to get him to quit talking about his home prepared in the world to come and his friend who came back from the dead.

· 25 ·

BELIEVE AND RECEIVE

Then they journeyed from Mount Hor by the Way of the
Red Sea, to go around the land of Edom; and the soul of
the people became very discouraged on the way. And the
people spoke against God and against Moses: "Why have you
brought us up out of Egypt to die in the wilderness? For there
is no food and no water, and our soul loathes this worthless
bread." So the LORD sent fiery serpents among the people, and
they bit the people; and many of the people of Israel died.

Therefore the people came to Moses, and said, "We
have sinned, for we have spoken against the LORD and
against you; pray to the LORD that He take away the
serpents from us." So Moses prayed for the people.

Then the LORD said to Moses, "Make a fiery serpent,
and set it on a pole; and it shall be that everyone who is
bitten, when he looks at it, shall live." So Moses made a
bronze serpent, and put it on a pole; and so it was, if a
serpent had bitten anyone, when he looked at the bronze
serpent, he lived.

—NUMBERS 21:4–9 NKJV

The wandering Israelites were grumbling at Moses again. Though camped on the border of the Promised Land, and beneficiaries of four decades of God's provisions, the Hebrews sound off like spoiled trust fund brats: "Why have you brought us up out of Egypt to die in the wilderness?" (Num. 21:5 NKJV).

Same complaint, seventieth verse. Ex-slaves longing for Egypt. Dreaming of pyramids and cursing the wasteland, pining for Pharaoh and vilifying Moses. They hate the hot sand, the long days, and the manna, oh the manna. "Our soul loathes this worthless bread" (v. 5 NKJV).

They've had all the manna burgers and manna casseroles and manna peanut butter sandwiches they can stomach. And, God has had all the moaning he can take. "So the LORD sent fiery serpents among the people, and they bit the people; and many of the people of Israel died" (v. 6 NKJV).

Horror movie producers long to spawn such scenes. Slithering vipers creep out of holes and rocks and snake through the camp. People die. Corpses dot the landscape. Survivors plead to Moses to plead to God for mercy.

"We have sinned . . . pray to the LORD that he take away the serpents from us." So Moses prayed for the people.

Then the LORD said to Moses, "Make a fiery serpent, and set it on a pole; and it shall be that everyone who is bitten, when he looks at it, shall live. So Moses made a bronze serpent, and put it on a pole; and so it was, if a serpent had bitten anyone, when he looked at the bronze serpent he lived" (vv. 7–9 NKJV).

This passage was a solemn prophecy.

And it was also a simple promise. Snake-bit Israelites found healing by looking to the pole. Sinners will find healing by looking to Christ. "Everyone who believes in him will have eternal life" (John 3:15 NLT 2007).

The simplicity troubles many people. We'd expect a more complicated cure, a more elaborate treatment. Moses and his followers might have expected more as well. Manufacture an ointment. Invent a therapeutic lotion. Treat one another. Or, at least, fight back. Break out the sticks and stones and attack the snakes.

We, too, expect a more proactive assignment, to have to conjure up a remedy for our sin. Some mercy seekers have donned hairshirts, climbed cathedral steps on their knees, or traversed hot rocks on bare feet.

Others of us have written our own Bible verse, "God helps those who help themselves" (Popular Opinion 1:1). We'll fix ourselves, thank you. We'll make up for our mistakes with contributions, our guilt with busyness, overcome failures with hard work. We'll find salvation the old-fashioned way; we'll earn it.

Christ, in contrast, says . . . "Your part is to trust. Trust me to do what you can't."

By the way, you take similar steps of trust daily, even hourly. You believe the chair will support you, so you set your weight on it. You believe water will hydrate you, so you swallow it. You trust the work of the light switch, so you flip it. You have faith the doorknob will work, so you turn it.

You regularly trust power you cannot see to do a work you cannot accomplish. Jesus invites you to do the same with him.

Just him. Not Moses or any other leader. Not other snake-bitten souls. Not even you. You can't fix you. Look to Jesus . . . and believe.

. . . FOR THOSE
WHO HURT US

Show mercy, just as your Father shows mercy.

—LUKE 6:36

· 26 ·

THE POWER OF FORGIVENESS

If I, your Lord and Teacher, have washed your feet, you also
should wash each other's feet. I did this as an example so
that you should do as I have done for you.

— JOHN 13:14-15

Recently I shared a meal with some friends. A husband and wife wanted to tell me about a storm they were weathering. Through a series of events, she learned of an act of infidelity that had occurred over a decade ago. He had made the mistake of thinking it'd be better not to tell her, so he didn't. But she found out. And as you can imagine, she was deeply hurt.

Through the advice of a counselor, the couple dropped everything and went away for several days. A decision had to be made. Would they flee, fight, or forgive? So they prayed. They talked. They walked. They reflected. In this case the wife was clearly in the right. She could have left. Women have done so for lesser reasons. Or she could have stayed and made his life a living hell. Other women have done that. But she chose a different response.

On the tenth night of their trip, my friend found a card on his pillow. On the card was a printed verse: "I'd rather do nothing with you than something without you." Beneath the verse she had written these words:

I forgive you. I love you. Let's move on.

The card might as well have been a basin. And the pen might as well have been a pitcher of water, for out of it poured pure mercy, and with it she washed her husband's feet.

Certain conflicts can be resolved only with a basin of water. Are any relationships in your world thirsty for mercy?

· 27 ·

THANKS FOR THE BREAD

When Jesus looked up and saw a large crowd coming toward him, he said to Philip, "Where can we buy enough bread for all these people to eat?" (Jesus asked Philip this question to test him, because Jesus already knew what he planned to do.)

Philip answered, "Someone would have to work almost a year to buy enough bread for each person to have only a little piece."

Another one of his followers, Andrew, Simon Peter's brother, said, "Here is a boy with five loaves of barley bread and two little fish, but that is not enough for so many people."

Jesus said, "Tell the people to sit down." There was plenty of grass there, and about five thousand men sat down there. Then Jesus took the loaves of bread, thanked God for them, and gave them to the people who were sitting there. He did the same with the fish, giving as much as the people wanted.

When they had all had enough to eat, Jesus said to his followers, "Gather the leftover pieces of fish and bread so that nothing is wasted." So they gathered up the pieces and filled twelve baskets with the pieces left from the five barley loaves.

When the people saw this miracle that Jesus did, they said, "He must truly be the Prophet who is coming into the world."

—JOHN 6:5-14

D ear friend,

I'm writing to say thanks. I wish I could thank you personally, but I don't know where you are. I wish I could call you, but I don't know your name. If I knew your appearance, I'd look for you, but your face is fuzzy in my memory. But I'll never forget what you did.

There you were, leaning against your pickup in the West Texas oil field. An engineer of some sort. A supervisor on the job. Your khakis and clean shirt set you apart from us roustabouts. In the oil field pecking order, we were at the bottom. You were the boss. We were the workers. You read the blueprints. We dug the ditches. You inspected the pipe. We laid it. You ate with the bosses in the shed. We ate with each other in the shade.

Except that day.

I remember wondering why you did it.

We weren't much to look at. What wasn't sweaty was oily. Faces burnt from the sun; skin black from the grease. Didn't bother me, though. I was there only for the summer. A high school boy earning good money laying pipe. For me, it was a summer job. For the others, it was a way of life. Most were illegal immigrants from Mexico. Others were drifters, bouncing across the prairie as rootless as tumbleweeds.

We weren't much to listen to, either. Our language was sandpaper coarse. After lunch, we'd light the cigarettes and begin the jokes. Someone always had a deck of cards with lacy-clad girls on the back. For thirty minutes in the heat of the day, the oil patch became Las Vegas—replete with foul language, dirty stories, blackjack, and barstools that doubled as lunch pails.

In the middle of such a game, you approached us. I thought you had a job for us that couldn't wait another few minutes. Like the others, I groaned when I saw you coming.

You were nervous. You shifted your weight from one leg to the other as you began to speak.

"Uh, fellows," you started.

We turned and looked up at you.

"I, uh, I just wanted, uh, to invite . . . "

You were way out of your comfort zone. I had no idea what you might be about to say, but I knew that it had nothing to do with work.

"I just wanted to tell you that, uh, our church is having a service tonight and, uh . . . "

"What?" I couldn't believe it. "He's talking church? Out here? With us?"

"I wanted to invite any of you to come along."

Silence. Screaming silence. The same silence you'd hear if a nun asked a madam if she could use the brothel for a mass.

The same silence you'd hear if an IRS representative invited the Mafia to a seminar on tax integrity.

Several guys stared at the dirt. A few shot glances at the others. Snickers rose just inches from the surface.

"Well, that's it. Uh, if any of you want to go . . . uh, let me know."

After you turned and left, we turned and laughed. We called you "reverend," "preacher," and "the pope." We poked fun at each other, daring one another to go. You became the butt of the day's jokes.

I'm sure you knew that. I'm sure you went back to your truck knowing the only good you'd done was to make a good fool out of yourself. If that's what you thought, then you were wrong.

That's the reason for this letter.

I thought of you this week. I thought of you when I read about someone else who took a risk at lunch. I thought of you when I read the story of the little boy who gave his lunch to Jesus (John 6:1–14).

His lunch wasn't much. In fact, it wasn't anything compared to what was needed for more than five thousand people.

He probably wrestled with the silliness of it all. What was one lunch for so many? He probably asked himself if it was even worth the effort.

How far could one lunch go?

I think that's why he didn't give the lunch to the crowd. Instead he gave it to Jesus. Something told him that if he would plant the seed, God would grant the crop.

So he did.

166

He summoned his courage, got up off the grass, and walked into the circle of grownups. He was as out of place in that cluster as you were in ours. He must have been nervous. No one likes to appear silly.

Someone probably snickered at him too.

If they didn't snicker, they shook their heads. "The little fellow doesn't know any better."

If they didn't shake their heads, they rolled their eyes. "Here we have a hunger crisis, and this little boy thinks that a sack lunch will solve it."

But it wasn't the men's heads or eyes that the boy saw; he saw only Jesus.

You must have seen Jesus, too, when you made your decision. Most people would have considered us to be unlikely deacon material. Most would have saved their seeds for softer soil. And they'd have been almost right. But Jesus said to give . . . so you gave.

As I think about it, you and the little boy have a lot in common:

- You both used your lunch to help others.
- You both chose faith over logic.
- You both brought a smile to your Father's face.

There's one difference, though. The boy got to see what Jesus did with his gift, and you didn't. That's why I'm writing. I want you to know that at least one of the seeds fell into a fertile crevice.

Some five years later, a college sophomore was struggling with a decision. He had drifted from the faith given to him by his parents. He wanted to come back. He wanted to come home. But the price was high. His friends might laugh. His habits would have to change. His reputation would have to be overcome.

Could he do it? Did he have the courage?

That's when I thought of you. As I sat in my dorm room late one night, looking for the guts to do what I knew was right, I thought of you.

I thought of how your love for God had been greater than your love for your reputation.

I thought of how your obedience had been greater than your common sense.

I remembered how you had cared more about making disciples than about making a good first impression. And when I thought of you, your memory became my motivation.

So I came home.

I've told your story dozens of times to thousands of people. Each time the reaction is the same: the audience becomes a sea of smiles, and heads bob in understanding. Some smile because they think of the "clean-shirted engineers" in their lives. They remember the neighbor who brought the cake, the aunt who wrote the letter, the teacher who listened . . .

Others smile because they have done what you did. And they, too, wonder if their "lunchtime loyalty" was worth the effort.

You wondered that. What you did that day wasn't much. And I'm sure you walked away that day thinking that your efforts had been wasted.

They weren't.

So I'm writing to say thanks. Thanks for the example.

Thanks for the courage. Thanks for giving your lunch to God. He did something with it; it became the Bread of Life for me.

Gratefully,

Max

P.S. If by some remarkable coincidence you read this and remember that day, please give me a call. I owe you lunch.

· 28 ·

WHEN YOU GET
BOOTED OUT

*The LORD said to [Hosea] again, "Go, show your love to a
woman loved by someone else, who has been unfaithful to you."*

—HOSEA 3:1

God will not let you go. He has handcuffed himself to you
in love. And he owns the only key. You need not win his
love. You already have it. And since you can't win it, you can't
lose it.

As evidence, consider exhibit A: the stubborn love of Hosea
for Gomer. Contrary to the name, Gomer was a female, an
irascible woman married to a remarkable Hosea. She had the
fidelity code of a prairie jackrabbit, flirting and hopping from
one lover to another. She ruined her life and shattered Hosea's
heart. Destitute, she was placed for sale in a slave market. Guess

who stepped forward to buy her? Hosea, who'd never removed his wedding band. The way he treated her you would have thought she'd never loved another man. God uses this story, indeed orchestrated this drama, to illustrate his steadfast love for his fickle people.

> Then GOD ordered [Hosea], "Start all over: Love your wife again,
>> your wife who's in bed with her latest boyfriend, your cheating wife.
> Love her the way I, GOD, love the Israelite people,
>> even as they flirt and party with every god that takes their fancy." (Hosea 3:1 MSG)

This is the love described in John 3:16. *Hasaq* is replaced with the Greek term *agape*, but the meaning is equally powerful. "God so [*agapao*] the world . . ."

Agape love. Less an affection, more a decision; less a feeling, more an action. As one linguist describes, "[Agape love is] an exercise of the Divine will in deliberate choice, made without assignable cause save that which lies in the nature of God Himself."[1]

Stated more simply: junkyard wrecks and showroom models share equal space in God's garage.

29

WHEN CRICKETS
MAKE YOU CRANKY

*After Jacob died, Joseph's brothers said, "What if Joseph
is still angry with us? We did many wrong things to him.
What if he plans to pay us back?" So they sent a message to
Joseph that said, "Your father gave this command before he
died. He said to us, 'You have done wrong and have sinned
and done evil to Joseph. Tell Joseph to forgive you, his
brothers.' So now, Joseph, we beg you to forgive our wrong.
We are the servants of the God of your father." When
Joseph received the message, he cried.*

*And his brothers went to him and bowed low before
him and said, "We are your slaves."*

*Then Joseph said to them, "Don't be afraid. Can I do
what only God can do? You meant to hurt me, but God
turned your evil into good to save the lives of many people,
which is being done. So don't be afraid. I will take care of
you and your children." So Joseph comforted his brothers and
spoke kind words to them.*

—GENESIS 50:15-21

Forgive me if this chapter is disjointed. As I write, I am angry. I am angered by a cricket. He's loud. He's obnoxious. He's hidden. And he's in big trouble if I ever find him.

I arrived at my office early. Two hours before my alarm sounded, I was here. Sleeves rolled back and computer humming. *Beat the phones*, I thought. *Get a jump on the morning*, I planned. *Get a leg up on the day.*

But "Get your hands on that cricket" is what I keep mumbling.

Now, I have nothing against nature. The melody of a canary, I love. The pleasant hum of the wind in the leaves, I relish. But the predawn *raack-raack-raack* of a cricket bugs me.

So I get on my knees and follow the sound through the office. I peek under boxes. I pull books off the shelves. I get on my belly and look under my desk. Humbling. I've been sabotaged by a one-inch bug.

What is this insolent irritant that reduces a man to bug-stalker?

Finally, I isolate the culprit.

Rats, he's behind a shelf. Out of my reach. Hidden in a haven of plywood. I can't get to him. All I can do is throw pens at the base of the shelf. So I do. *Pop. Pop. Pop.* One after another. A barrage of Bics. He finally shuts up.

But the silence lasts only a minute.

So forgive me if my thoughts are fragmented, but I'm launching artillery every-other paragraph. This is no way to work. This is no way to start the day. My floor is cluttered. My pants are dirty. My train of thought is derailed. I mean, how can you write about anger with a stupid bug in your office?

Oooops. Guess I'm in the right frame of mind after all . . .

Anger. This morning it's easy to define: the noise of the soul. *Anger.* The unseen irritant of the heart. *Anger.* The relentless invader of silence.

Just like the cricket, anger irritates.

Just like the cricket, anger isn't easily silenced.

Just like the cricket, anger has a way of increasing in volume until it's the only sound we hear. The louder it gets, the more desperate we become.

When we are mistreated, our animalistic response is to go on the hunt. Instinctively, we double up our fists. Getting even is only natural. Which, incidentally, is precisely the problem. Revenge is natural, not spiritual. Getting even is the rule of the jungle. Giving grace is the rule of the kingdom.

Some of you are thinking, *Easy for you to say, Max, sitting there in your office with a cricket as your chief irritant. You ought to try living with my wife.* Or, *You ought to have to cope with my past.* Or, *You ought to raise my kids. You don't know how my ex has mistreated me. You don't have any idea how hard my life has been.*

And you're right, I don't. But I have a very clear idea how miserable your future will be unless you deal with your anger.

X-ray the soul of the vengeful and behold the tumor of bitterness: black, menacing, malignant. Carcinoma of the spirit. Its fatal fibers creep around the edge of the heart and ravage it. Yesterday you can't alter, but your reaction to yesterday you can. The past you cannot change, but your response to your past you can.

Impossible, you say? Let me try to show you otherwise.

Imagine you are from a large family—a dozen or so kids. A family more blended than the Brady bunch. All the children are from the same dad, but they have four or five different moms.

Imagine also that your dad is a sneak and has been one for a long time. Everybody knows it. Everybody knows he cheated your uncle out of the estate. Everybody knows he ran like a coward to avoid getting caught.

Let's also imagine that your great-uncle tricked your dad into marrying your mother's sister. He got your dad drunk before the wedding and had his ugly daughter go to the altar instead of the pretty one your dad thought he was marrying.

That didn't slow down your father, though. He just married them both. The one he loved couldn't have kids, so he slept with her maid. In fact, he had a habit of sleeping with most of the kitchen help; as a result, most of your siblings resemble the cooks.

Finally the bride your dad wanted to marry in the first place gets pregnant . . . and you are born.

You're the favored son . . . and your brothers know it.

You get a car. They don't. You get Armani; they get K-Mart. You get summer camp; they get summer jobs. You get educated; they get angry.

And they get even. They sell you to some foreign service project, put you on a plane for Egypt, and tell your dad you got shot by a sniper. You find yourself surrounded by people you don't know, learning a language you don't understand, and living in a culture you've never seen.

Imaginary tale? No. It's the story of Joseph. A favored son in a bizarre family, he had every reason to be angry.

He tried to make the best of it. He became the chief servant of the head of the Secret Service. His boss's wife tried to seduce him, and when he refused, she pouted and he ended up in prison. Pharaoh got wind of the fact that Joseph could interpret dreams and let him take a shot at some of Pharaoh's own.

When Joseph interpreted them he got promoted out of the prison into the palace as prime minister. The second-highest position in all of Egypt. The only person Joseph bowed before was the king.

Meanwhile a famine hits and Jacob, Joseph's father, sends his sons to Egypt for a foreign loan. The brothers don't know it, but they are standing in front of the same brother they sold to the gypsies some twenty-two years earlier.

They don't recognize Joseph, but Joseph recognizes them. A bit balder and paunchier, but they are the same brothers. Imagine Joseph's thoughts. The last time he saw these faces, he was looking up at them from the bottom of a pit. The last time he heard these voices, they were laughing at him. The last time they called his name, they called him every name in the book.

Now is his chance to get even. He has complete control. One snap of his fingers and these brothers are dead. Better yet, slap some manacles on their hands and feet and let them see what an Egyptian dungeon is like. Let them sleep in the mud. Let them mop floors. Let them learn Egyptian.

Revenge is within Joseph's power. And there is power in revenge. Intoxicating power.

Haven't we tasted it? Haven't we been tempted to get even?

As we escort the offender into the courtroom, we announce,

"He hurt me!" The jurors shake their heads in disgust. "He abandoned me!" we explain, and the chambers echo with our accusation. "Guilty!" the judge snarls as he slams the gavel. "Guilty!" the jury agrees. "Guilty!" the audience proclaims. We delight in this moment of justice. We relish this pound of flesh. So we prolong the event. We tell the story again and again and again.

Now let's freeze-frame that scene. I have a question. Not for all of you, but for a few of you. Some of you are in the courtroom. The courtroom of complaint. Some of you are rehashing the same hurt every chance you get with anyone who will listen.

For you, I have this question: Who made you God? I don't mean to be cocky, but why are you doing his work for him?

"Vengeance is Mine," God declared. "I will repay" (Heb. 10:30 NKJV).

"Don't say, 'I'll pay you back for the wrong you did.' / Wait for the LORD, and he will make things right" (Prov. 20:22).

Judgment is God's job. To assume otherwise is to assume God can't do it.

Revenge is irreverent. When we strike back we are saying, "I know vengeance is yours, God, but I just didn't think you'd punish enough. I thought I'd better take this situation into my own hands. You have a tendency to be a little soft."

Joseph understands that. Rather than get even, he reveals his identity and has his father and the rest of the family brought to Egypt. He grants them safety and provides them a place to live. They live in harmony for seventeen years.

But then Jacob dies and the moment of truth comes. The brothers have a hunch that with Jacob gone they'll be lucky to get out of Egypt with their heads on their shoulders. So they go to Joseph and plead for mercy.

"Your father gave this command before he died. . . . 'Tell Joseph to forgive you'" (Gen. 50:16–17). (I have to smile at the thought of grown men talking like this. Don't they sound like kids, whining, "Daddy said to be nice to us"?)

Joseph's response? "When Joseph received the message, he cried" (Gen. 50:17). *What more do I have to do?* his tears implore. *I've given you a home. I've provided for your families. Why do you still mistrust my grace?*

Please read carefully the two statements he makes to his brothers. First he asks, "Can I do what only God can do?" (v. 19).

May I restate the obvious? Revenge belongs to God! If vengeance is God's, then it is not ours. God has not asked us to settle the score or get even. Ever.

Why? The answer is found in the second part of Joseph's statement: "You meant to hurt me, but God turned your evil into good to save the lives of many people, which is being done" (v. 20).

Forgiveness comes easier with a wide-angle lens. Joseph uses one to get the whole picture. He refuses to focus on the betrayal of his brothers without also seeing the loyalty of his God.

It always helps to see the big picture.

Some time ago I was in an airport lobby when I saw an acquaintance enter. He was a man I hadn't seen in a while but had thought about often. He'd been through a divorce, and I was close enough to it to know that he deserved some of the blame.

I noticed he was not alone. Beside him was a woman. *Why, that scoundrel! Just a few months out and here he has another lady?*

Any thought of greeting him disappeared as I passed judgment on his character. But then he saw me. He waved at me. He motioned me over. I was caught. I was trapped. I'd have to go visit with the reprobate. So I did.

"Max, meet my aunt and her husband."

I gulped. I hadn't noticed the man.

"We're on our way to a family reunion. I know they would really like to meet you."

"We use your books in our home Bible study," my friend's uncle spoke up. "You've got some great insights."

"If only you knew," I said to myself. I had committed a common sin of the unforgiving. I had cast a vote without knowing the story.

To forgive someone is to admit our limitations. We've been given only one piece of life's jigsaw puzzle. Only God has the cover of the box.

To forgive someone is to display reverence. Forgiveness is not saying the one who hurt you was right. Forgiveness is stating that God is fair and he will do what is right.

After all, don't we have enough things to do without trying to do God's work too?

Guess what. I just noticed something. The cricket is quiet. I got so wrapped up in this chapter I forgot him. I haven't thrown a pen for an hour. Guess he fell asleep. Could be that's what he wanted to do all along, but I kept waking him up with my Bics.

He ended up getting some rest. I ended up finishing this chapter. Remarkable what gets accomplished when we let go of our anger.

30

THE FATHER IN THE
FACE OF THE ENEMY

Be kind and loving to each other, and forgive each other
just as God forgave you in Christ.

—EPHESIANS 4:32

Daniel is big. He used to make his living by lifting weights and teaching others to do the same. His scrapbook is colorful with ribbons and photos of him in his prime, striking the muscle-man pose and flexing the bulging arms.

The only thing bigger than Daniel's biceps is his heart. Let me tell you about a time his heart became tender.

Daniel was living in the southern city of Porto Alegre. He worked at a gym and dreamed of owning his own. The bank agreed to finance the purchase if he could find someone to cosign the note. His brother agreed.

They filled out all the applications and awaited the approval. Everything went smoothly, and Daniel soon received a call from the bank telling him he could come and pick up the check. As soon as he got off work, he went to the bank.

When the loan officer saw Daniel, he looked surprised and asked Daniel why he had come.

"To pick up the check," Daniel explained.

"That's funny," responded the banker. "Your brother was in here earlier. He picked up the money and used it to retire the mortgage on his house."

Daniel was incensed. He never dreamed his own brother would trick him like that. He stormed over to his brother's house and pounded on the door. The brother answered the door with his daughter in his arms. He knew Daniel wouldn't hit him if he was holding a child.

He was right. Daniel didn't hit him. But he promised his brother that if he ever saw him again he would break his neck.

Daniel went home, his big heart bruised and ravaged by the trickery of his brother. He had no other choice but to go back to the gym and work to pay off the debt.

A few months later, Daniel met a young American missionary named Allen Dutton. Allen befriended Daniel and taught him about Jesus Christ. Daniel and his wife soon became Christians and devoted disciples.

But though Daniel had been forgiven so much, he still found it impossible to forgive his brother. The wound was deep. The pot of revenge still simmered. He didn't see his brother for two years. Daniel couldn't bring himself to look into the face of the one who had betrayed him. And his brother liked his own face too much to let Daniel see it.

But an encounter was inevitable. Both knew they would eventually run into each other. And neither knew what would happen then.

The encounter occurred one day on a busy avenue. Let Daniel tell you in his own words what happened:

> I saw him, but he didn't see me. I felt my fists clench and my face get hot. My initial impulse was to grab him around the throat and choke the life out of him.
>
> But as I looked into his face, my anger began to melt. For as I saw him, I saw the image of my father. I saw my father's eyes. I saw my father's look. I saw my father's expression. And as I saw my father in his face, my enemy once again became my brother.

Daniel walked toward him. The brother stopped, turned, and started to run, but he was too slow. Daniel reached out and grabbed his shoulder. The brother winced, expecting the worst. But rather than have his throat squeezed by Daniel's hands, he found himself hugged by Daniel's big arms. And the two brothers stood in the middle of the river of people and wept.

Daniel's words are worth repeating: "As I saw my father in his face, my enemy once again became my brother."

Seeing the father's image in the face of the enemy. Try that. The next time you see or think of the one who broke your heart, look twice. As you look at his face, look also for his face—the face of the One who forgave you. Look into the eyes of the King who wept when you pleaded for mercy. Look into the face of the Father who gave you grace when no one else gave you a chance. Find the face of the God who forgives in the face of your enemy. And then, because God has forgiven you more than you'll ever be called on to forgive in another, set your enemy—and yourself—free.

And allow the hole in your heart to heal.

NOTES

Chapter 4: I Will Not Abandon You

1. "If you, then, though you are evil, know how to give good gifts to your children, how much more will your Father in heaven give good gifts to those who ask him!" (Matt. 7:11 NIV).
2. Frank Stagg, *New Testament Theology* (Nashville: Broadman Press, 1962), 102.

Chapter 7: Two Tombstones

1. This story is found in John 4:1–42.

Chapter 9: Guilt or Grace

1. James F. Colianni, *The Book of Pulpit Humor* (Ventnor, NJ: Voicings Publications, 1992), 128.

Chapter 13: Dressed in His Righteousness Alone

1. Edward Mote, "The Solid Rock."

Chapter 15: Tank Your Reputation

1. Scot McKnight, *The Jesus Creed: Loving God, Loving Others* (Brewster, MA: Paraclete Press, 2004), 77.
2. The Jewish confession of faith, comprising Deuteronomy 6:4–9; 11:13–21; and Numbers 15:37–41.

Chapter 20: When Grace Goes Deep

1. Ron Lee Davis with James D. Denny, *Mistreated* (Portland, OR: Multnomah Press, 1989), 147–48.

NOTES

Chapter 21: What We Really Want to Know

1. Steven Cole, "Forgiveness," *Leadership Magazine*, 1983, 86.

Chapter 28: When You Get Booted Out

1. W. E. Vine, *Expository Dictionary of New Testament Words: A Comprehensive Dictionary of the Original Greek Words with Their Precise Meanings for English Readers* (McClean, VA: MacDonald Publishing Company, n.d.), 703.

SOURCES

The chapters in this book were originally published in books authored by Max Lucado. All copyrights to the original works are held by Max Lucado.

. . . For the Rebellious

Chapter 1: Open Arms: *Six Hours, One Friday*, chapter 11.
Chapter 2: Come Home: *No Wonder They Call Him the Savior*, chapter 31.
Chapter 3: Bright Lights on Dark Nights: *He Still Moves Stones*, chapter 11.
Chapter 4: I Will Not Abandon You: *He Chose the Nails*, chapter 7.
Chapter 5: The Golden Goblet: *Six Hours One Friday*, chapter 10.
Chapter 6: Nearer Than You've Dreamed: *Come Thirsty*, "Meagan."

. . . For the Regret-Riddled

Chapter 7: Two Tombstones: *Six Hours One Friday*, chapter 3.
Chapter 8: The Voice from the Mop Bucket: *When God Whispers Your Name*, chapter 1.
Chapter 9: Guilt or Grace: *A Gentle Thunder*, chapter 27.
Chapter 10: The Eleventh Hour Gift: *Six Hours One Friday*, chapter 13.
Chapter 11: Imperfect People: *Next Door Savior*, chapter 10.

. . . For the Prideful

Chapter 12: The Kingdom of the Absurd: *The Applause of Heaven*, chapter 4.
Chapter 13: Dressed in His Righteousness Alone: *In the Grip of Grace*, Introduction.
Chapter 14: Where Man Covers His Mouth: *The Great House of God*, chapter 5.

Chapter 15: Tank Your Reputation: *Cure for the Common Life*, chapter 10.

... For the Mistake-Makers

Chapter 16: The Tenderness of God: *He Still Moves Stones*, chapter 15.

Chapter 17: Puppies, Butterflies, and a Savior: *No Wonder They Call Him the Savior*, chapter 27.

Chapter 18: Not Guilty: *He Still Moves Stones*, chapter 2.

Chapter 19: The Ring of Belief: *A Love Worth Giving*, chapter 13.

Chapter 20: When Grace Goes Deep: *Come Thirsty*, chapter 3.

Chapter 21: What We Really Want to Know: *In the Grip of Grace*, chapter 17.

... For a Faltering Faith

Chapter 22: The Gospel of the Second Chance: *No Wonder They Call Him the Savior*, chapter 17.

Chapter 23: Remember: *Six Hours One Friday*, chapter 7.

Chapter 24: Leave Room for the Magic: *No Wonder They Call Him the Savior*, chapter 18.

Chapter 25: Believe and Receive: *3:16: The Numbers of Hope*, chapter 8.

... For Those Who Hurt Us

Chapter 26: The Power of Forgiveness: *Just Like Jesus*, chapter 2.

Chapter 27: Thanks for the Bread: *In the Eye of the Storm*, chapter 7.

Chapter 28: When You Get Booted Out: *3:16, The Numbers of Hope*, chapter 4.

Chapter 29: When Crickets Make You Cranky: *When God Whispers Your Name*, chapter 13.

Chapter 30: The Father in the Face of the Enemy: *The Applause of Heaven*, chapter 11.

ᴃ The Lucado Reader's Guide ᴃ

Discover . . . Inside every book by Max Lucado, you'll find words of
encouragement and inspiration that will draw you into a deeper experience with
Jesus and treasures for your walk with God. What will you discover?

3:16: The Numbers of Hope
… the 26 words that can change
your life.
core scripture: John 3:16

And the Angels Were Silent
… what Jesus Christ's final days can
teach you about what matters most.
core scripture: Matthew 20–27

The Applause of Heaven
… the secret to a truly satisfying
life.
core scripture: The Beatitudes,
Matthew 5:1–10

Come Thirsty
… how to rehydrate your heart
and sink into the wellspring of
God's love.
core scripture: John 7:37–38

Cure for the Common Life
… the unique things God designed
you to do with your life.
core scripture: 1 Corinthians 12:7

Facing Your Giants
… when God is for you,
no challenge is too great.
core scripture: 1 and 2 Samuel

Fearless
… how faith is the antidote to
the fear in your life.
core scripture: John 14:1, 3

A Gentle Thunder
… the God who will do whatever
it takes to lead his children back
to him.
core scripture: Psalm 81:7

Great Day, Every Day
… how living in a purposeful way
will help you trust more, stress less.
core scripture: Psalm 118:24

The Great House of God
… a blueprint for peace, joy, and
love found in the Lord's Prayer.
core scripture: The Lord's Prayer,
Matthew 6:9–13

God Came Near
… a love so great that it left heaven
to become part of your world.
core scripture: John 1:14

He Chose the Nails
… a love so deep that it chose death
on a cross—just to win your heart.
core scripture: 1 Peter 1:18–20

He Still Moves Stones
… the God who still does the
impossible—in your life.
core scripture: Matthew 12:20

In the Eye of the Storm
… peace in the storms of your life.
core scripture: John 6

In the Grip of Grace
… the greatest gift of all—the
grace of God.
core scripture: Romans

It's Not About Me
… why focusing on God will make
sense of your life.
core scripture: 2 Corinthians 3:18

Just Like Jesus
… a life free from guilt, fear,
and anxiety.
core scripture: Ephesians 4:23–24

A Love Worth Giving
… how living loved frees you
to love others.
core scripture: 1 Corinthians 13

Next Door Savior
… a God who walked life's
hardest trials—and still walks
with you through yours.
core scripture: Matthew 16:13–16

**No Wonder They Call Him
the Savior**
… hope in the unlikeliest place—
upon the cross.
core scripture: Romans 5:15

Outlive Your Life
… that a great God created you
to do great things.
core scripture: Acts 1

Six Hours One Friday
… forgiveness and healing in
the middle of loss and failure.
core scripture: John 19–20

Traveling Light
… the power to release the burdens
you were never meant to carry.
core scripture: Psalm 23

**When God Whispers
Your Name**
… the path to hope in knowing
that God knows you, never forgets
you, and cares about the details of
your life.
core scripture: John 10:3

When Christ Comes
… why the best is yet to come.
core scripture: 1 Corinthians 15:23

Recommended reading if you're struggling with . . .

FEAR AND WORRY
Come Thirsty
Fearless
For the Tough Times
Next Door Savior
Traveling Light

DISCOURAGEMENT
He Still Moves Stones
Next Door Savior

GRIEF/DEATH OF A LOVED ONE
Next Door Savior
Traveling Light
When Christ Comes
When God Whispers Your Name

GUILT
In the Grip of Grace
Just Like Jesus

LONELINESS
God Came Near

SIN
Facing Your Giants
He Chose the Nails
Six Hours One Friday

WEARINESS
When God Whispers Your Name

Recommended reading if you want to know more about . . .

THE CROSS
And the Angels Were Silent
He Chose the Nails
No Wonder They Call Him the Savior
Six Hours One Friday

GRACE
He Chose the Nails
In the Grip of Grace

HEAVEN
The Applause of Heaven
When Christ Comes

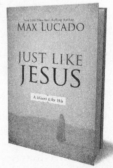

SHARING THE GOSPEL
God Came Near
No Wonder They Call Him the Savior

Recommended reading if you're looking for more . . .

COMFORT
For the Tough Times
He Chose the Nails
Next Door Savior
Traveling Light

JOY
The Applause of Heaven
Cure for the Common Life
When God Whispers Your Name

PEACE
And the Angels Were Silent
The Great House of God
In the Eye of the Storm
Traveling Light

COMPASSION
Outlive Your Life

SATISFACTION
And the Angels Were Silent
Come Thirsty
Cure for the Common Life
Great Day, Every Day

COURAGE
Facing Your Giants
Fearless

HOPE
3:16: The Numbers of Hope
Facing Your Giants
A Gentle Thunder
God Came Near

TRUST
A Gentle Thunder
It's Not About Me
Next Door Savior

LOVE
Come Thirsty
A Love Worth Giving
No Wonder They Call Him the Savior

Max Lucado books make great gifts!
If you're coming up to a special occasion, consider one of these.

FOR ADULTS:
For the Tough Times
Grace for the Moment
Live Loved
The Lucado Life Lessons Study Bible
Mocha with Max
DaySpring Daybrighteners® and cards

FOR TEENS/GRADUATES:
Let the Journey Begin
You Can Be Everything God Wants You to Be
You Were Made to Make a Difference

FOR KIDS:
Just in Case You Ever Wonder
The Oak Inside the Acorn
You Are Special

FOR PASTORS AND TEACHERS:
God Thinks You're Wonderful
You Changed My Life

AT CHRISTMAS:
The Crippled Lamb
Christmas Stories from Max Lucado
God Came Near

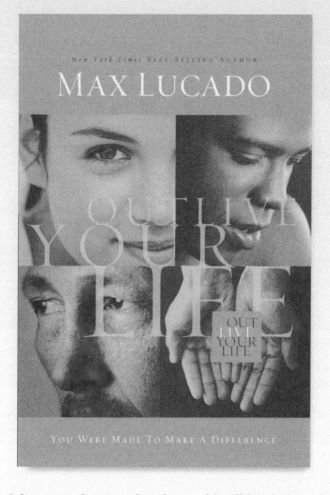

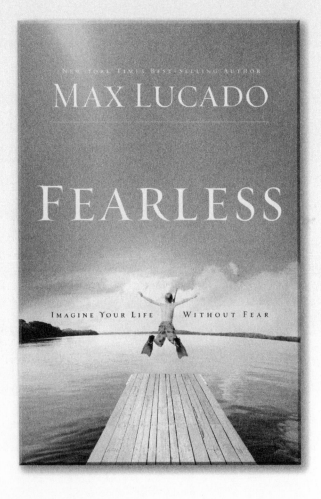

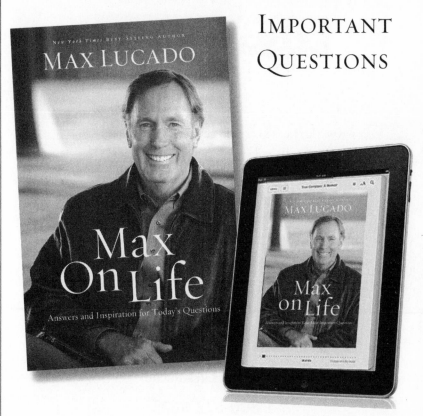

Inspired by what you just read?
Connect with Max.

Listen to Max's teaching ministry, UpWords, on the radio and online. Visit www.MaxLucado.com to get FREE resources for spiritual growth and encouragement, including:

- Archives of UpWords, Max's daily radio program, and a list of radio stations where it airs
- Devotionals and e-mails from Max
- First look at book excerpts
- Downloads of audio, video, and printed material
- Mobile content

You will also find an online store and special offers.

www.MaxLucado.com

1-800-822-9673

UpWords Ministries
P.O. Box 692170
San Antonio, TX 78269-2170

Join the Max Lucado community:

Follow Max on Twitter @MaxLucado
or at Facebook.com/MaxLucado